Appropriate Environr Children under Three

D0070931

The most rapid and significant phase of development occurs in the first three years of a child's life. The *Supporting Children from Birth to Three* series focuses on the care and support of the youngest children. Each book takes a key aspect of working with this age group and gives clear and detailed explanations of relevant theories together with practical examples to show how such theories translate into good working practice.

It is widely known that babies and infants will flourish in an environment that supports and promotes their learning and development. But what constitutes an appropriate environment for children under three?

Drawing on recent research, this book explores the concept of an appropriate environment, both within and beyond the early years setting. It sets this within the context of child development and practically demonstrates how a high-quality environment can be created for babies and children under three that supports their learning and development.

Features include:

- clear explanation of relevant theories
- case studies and examples of good practice
- focus points for readers
- questions for reflective practice

Providing a wealth of practical ideas and activities, this handy text provides detailed guidance on how to develop an appropriate indoor and outdoor environment for babies and children under three, to help practitioners ensure effective outcomes for the youngest children in their care.

Helen Bradford is an Early Years Tutor on the Early Years and Primary PGCE course at the Faculty of Education, University of Cambridge, UK. Her previous publications include: *Communication, Language and Literacy* (Fulton, 2008), *Bears* (Fulton, 2006), *Woodland Creatures* (Fulton, 2005) and *Ourselves* (Fulton, 2005).

Supporting Children from Birth to Three
Series Editor: Sandy Green

The most rapid and significant phase of development occurs in the first three years of a child's life. The *Supporting Children from Birth to Three* series focuses on the care and support of the youngest children. Each book takes a key aspect of working with this age group and gives clear and detailed explanations of relevant theories together with practical examples to show how such theories translate into good working practice.

Each title in this series includes the following features:

- clear explanation of relevant theories
- case studies and examples of good practice
- focus points for readers
- questions for reflective practice

Collectively, the series provides practical ideas and activities to help practitioners develop appropriate indoor and outdoor environments, appreciate the importance of the planning cycle and gain a better understanding of all aspects of babies' and infants' wellbeing.

Titles in this series include:

Appropriate Environments for Children under Three
Helen Bradford

Planning and Observation with Children under Three
Helen Bradford

The Wellbeing of Children under Three
Helen Bradford

Appropriate Environments for Children under Three

Helen Bradford

Routledge
Taylor & Francis Group

LONDON AND NEW YORK

HARVARD UNIVERSITY
GRADUATE SCHOOL OF EDUCATION
MONROE C. GUTMAN LIBRARY

First published 2012
by Routledge
2 Park Square, Milton Park, Abingdon, Oxon OX14 4RN

Simultaneously published in the USA and Canada
by Routledge
711 Third Avenue, New York, NY 10017

Routledge is an imprint of the Taylor & Francis Group, an informa business

© 2012 Helen Bradford

The right of Helen Bradford to be identified as author of this work has been
asserted by her in accordance with sections 77 and 78 of the Copyright,
Designs and Patents Act 1988.

All rights reserved. No part of this book may be reprinted or reproduced or
utilised in any form or by any electronic, mechanical, or other means, now
known or hereafter invented, including photocopying and recording, or in
any information storage or retrieval system, without permission in writing
from the publishers.

Trademark notice: Product or corporate names may be trademarks or
registered trademarks, and are used only for identification and explanation
without intent to infringe.

British Library Cataloguing in Publication Data
A catalogue record for this book is available from the British Library

Library of Congress Cataloging in Publication Data
Bradford, Helen.
  Appropriate environments for children under three / Helen Bradford.
    p. cm. — (Supporting children series)
  1. Early childhood education. 2. Child development. I. Title.
  LB1139.23.B73 2011
  372.21—dc22

                                                    2011008284

ISBN: 978-0-415-61262-3 (hbk)
ISBN: 978-0-415-61263-0 (pbk)
ISBN: 978-0-203-80495-7 (ebk)

Typeset in Optima
by FiSH Books, Enfield

MIX
Paper from
responsible sources
FSC® C004839

Printed and bound in Great Britain by
CPI Antony Rowe, Chippenham, Wiltshire

Contents

Introduction

Appropriate Environments for Children under Three is one of a series of three books providing supportive and accessible material for those working with the very youngest children, from birth to three years. The premise for all three books is twofold; all babies and young children are (a) social beings and (b) competent learners from birth. The other two titles in the series are: *Planning and Observation for Children under Three* and *The Wellbeing of Children under Three*.

The books are designed for all early years professionals and adults working with babies and children under three in their early years settings who are seeking ideas on how to optimise best practice using the space and resources they have available to them. The books explore some of the theories and principles behind good practice in each of the title areas outlined. *Appropriate Environments for Children under Three* includes case studies, examples from practice, and exercises entitled 'Reflecting on current practice', as well as a final chapter with suggestions for reviewing setting practice, including staff development. The series is written from the perspective of the early years practitioner as someone who is in a privileged position to work with children from birth to three; someone who is able to see and respond to each child they encounter as the individualistic person that they are. Thus, how can the early years practitioner working from such a perspective best meet children's individual needs? How can every child be best supported as they evolve to make sense of the world around them?

The books take a reflective, child-led approach where good practice begins with an understanding of child development, appropriate responses, honest evaluation and ongoing discourse amongst practitioners. *Appropriate Environments for Children under Three* relies on a staff team who can work collaboratively to develop ways of providing high-quality learning environments so that all the children in their care feel secure and happy and are able to thrive. This means, paradoxically, that children must also feel able to take risks appropriate to their stages of development; to explore, inquire, and experiment as their knowledge and understanding of the environments they inhabit grows. As they develop a language, or meta-language, that enables them to communicate in and navigate those environments, and as they develop the physical and creative skills necessary to experience the exciting and intriguing spaces that unfold before them, children begin a journey of understanding that will support and equip them for life ahead. According to the Early Childhood Forum, '[pre-school experience] is a crucial time in children's development... pre-school experience provides many of the building blocks for the rest of their lives.' The key message of this book, therefore, is that appropriate environments play a pivotal role in supporting and extending children's development and learning.

All five chapters build on each other, whilst containing the same core messages. Chapter 1 outlines a definition of an appropriate environment to include a wider perspective than merely that of the physical environment the child encounters within the early years setting. The definition encompasses the child's wider environment and key relationships within it. Chapter 2 gives an extensive overview of the developing child from birth to three years, linking theory with appropriate practice within the child's physical, social and emotional environment. Chapter 3 looks at what can be gleaned in relation to appropriate environments for babies and children under three through awareness of a global early years perspective. Chapter 4 extends the definition of inclusion beyond provision for children with special educational needs and learning disabilities, instead considering the necessity for children, families and staff to all feel that they are accepted and valued in order for the setting to thrive. Taking play as an example, it shows what aspects to consider in order to address inclusive practice, aspects that impact on what is meant by the considered development of an appropriate environment for learning. The final chapter offers a potential way forward for an early years setting to begin to review current practice, linking what we know about the specific and unique needs of babies and children under three with practical responses.

Figure 1 The happy child

Setting the scene: What is an appropriate environment?

This chapter explores the concept of what constitutes an appropriate environment for babies and children under three. It challenges the reader into a more holistic understanding of a term that encompasses and responds to the child's wider environment, both within and beyond the immediate early years setting. Within the early years setting, an appropriate environment includes all aspects of the indoor and outdoor environment and the responsiveness of that environment – including the adults who work there – in meeting the physical, emotional and learning needs of all the babies and children under three in their care. It is one where children are able to acquire new knowledge and understanding about their world or a new skill or behaviour as a result of experience. An appropriate environment for babies and children under three thus further encompasses the provision of developmentally appropriate care.

Providing the optimum early years environment

The physical environment of the preschool setting should reflect knowledge of and respect for the safety, physical wellbeing, intellectual stimulation, and social support of the very young...environments for young children should always reflect concern for all aspects of child development; physical, intellectual, social, and emotional. Space and materials...should enhance socialness, support a sense of emotional safety, and reflect respect for the familial and cultural experiences of the child. It is imperative that the transition from home to school should not be so drastic as

> to cause psychological or emotional stress by imposing rigid sched-
> ules, long periods of sedentary activity, confined spaces, unsafe
> equipment, or intense academic pressures on young children.
>
> (Renck Jalongo *et al.*, 2004: 144)

A major context for this book develops from an approach that recognises that babies and children under three have unique characteristics, behave in particular ways and have specialised needs. A number of educators have, over time, defined the 'ideal' early years learning environment. Child-centred approaches, particularly Froebelian, were based on the notion that a child's inborn characteristics must be allowed to flower; 'to make the inner outer' (Seefeldt and Barbour, 1998, cited in Li, 2006: 37). Froebel believed that the early years educator should provide opportunities for spontaneous play. Susan Isaacs, on the other hand, outlined the importance of leaving children free to choose their own form of expression. This line of thinking continues with Holt's (1989) argument that real learning is not the result of direct teaching, but the outcome of working things out for oneself.

Many early childhood educators such as Froebel, Montessori, Isaacs, Steiner, Vygotsky, Piaget and Bruner based their theories upon the view that children learn to make sense of the world by building up concepts through interaction with their environments (Moyles, 1997). Following on from such theories of what constitutes good early years practice, today's early years practitioner is expected to start from a child's everyday understanding and construction of knowledge of their immediate surrounding world and to discover and create opportunities to support and scaffold their active explo-ration of it. Active learning has been acknowledged as crucial to the cognitive and other developmental processes of young children (Moyles, 1997). Children learn as they make physical and mental connections with the world through sensory exploration, personal effort and social experiences, and actively seek meanings from those experiences. The purpose of care and education is therefore to help the child achieve higher levels of development through interactions with their physical and social environments.

The first nursery school in the UK was established in 1816 in New Lanark, Scotland, by the social reformer Robert Owen. It formed part of the Institution, which was a place of support, community and education for families. The Institution offered a variety of services including parenting classes and employment training as well as an academic education. It was also set up to ensure social inclusion. In England, almost 200 years later, the 2006 Childcare Act underpins the statutory provision of early years services and children's centres for babies and children up to the age of 5, services regulated to deliver a similar ethos of integrated provision. Local authorities are required to (a) ensure that they provide sufficient childcare to enable parents to work, and (b) improve outcomes for young children through targeted early years provision in their area, with the remit to narrow the gap between those children who do well and those who do not (Alexander, 2010). The concept of 'provision in their area' is important because it recognises that, in this country at least, people often live in culturally diverse communities. Whilst local authorities might operate under a blanket policy framework, this must remain somewhat open to interpretation. There has to be an element of flexibility involved as any early years provision should be tailored to meet the specific needs of each community, an approach important for the identity of each early years setting which should be perceived as a community in itself.

As suggested, the two above-mentioned requirements for local authorities are not necessarily new concepts. The following quotation, taken from Owen's Address to the Inhabitants of New Lanark, outlines the role of the nursery school at his Institution:

> to afford the means of receiving your children at an early age, almost as soon as they can walk. By this means many of you, mothers and families, will be able to earn a better maintenance or support for your children; you will have less care and anxiety about them, while the children will be prevented from acquiring any bad habits and gradually prepared to learn the best.
> (Address to the Inhabitants of New Lanark, New Year's Day, 1816)

Quite what Owen meant by 'bad habits' one can only speculate. Perhaps it is about expectations surrounding what it means to be a good citizen. Or was it that his far-reaching thinking perceived the nursery to be an appropriate environment for these very young children, a setting advantageous, in many ways, for them to participate in? The nursery was, perhaps, somewhere to support these children in their early years, to equip them with the necessary skills in order to be able to succeed in later life. The sentiment behind his message is clear enough, however; it is one of appropriate support in an appropriate environment, somewhere that meets the needs of its attendees. It is in this appropriate environment that one is 'gradually prepared to learn the best'. This is important, as we will discover further in this book, in relation to a child's particular stage of development.

Providing the optimum early years environment: the case for a key worker approach

Babies and children under three thrive on consistency; for example consistency of routine and of familiar places and patterns, both at home and in their early years setting. Consistency within the early years setting suggests an environment that is regular, predictable and constant. This should extend to include regularity, predictability and constancy of relationships. A major element of provision of consistency within the early years environment can be offered through the key worker approach, an approach in which one person assumes overall care and responsibility for a child. A key worker is someone with whom the child can form a secure, trusting relationship. Whilst in practice many tasks within the setting may be shared by more than one person, the intention should be that as much as is feasible should be carried out by the key worker. A key worker is likely to assume overall responsibility for a group of key children. Noddings (2002: 178–9) argues that, 'we would all prefer to be cared for by someone who enjoys our company rather than by someone who acts out of grim duty'. Babies 'learn best by playing with the things they find in their world, and above all by playing with the familiar people who love them' (David et al., 2003: 150). Key workers should be practitioners who are experts in their field. They are specialists who understand and respond to babies' and young children's needs, both physical and emotional; specialists who can support developing social skills, who interact willingly with the children in their care and who share conversations fuelled by mutual enjoyment of genuinely shared interests. Specialist practitioners know how to develop the early years environment to support young children's individual needs.

An effective key worker approach supports the following benefits for babies and children under three:

- promoting healthy emotional attachments with a child by providing familiar, trusting, safe and secure relationships. The key worker is the person who knows the child well and is aware of all the special details of how they are cared for, helping them to feel cherished and able to express themselves fully, to relax and feel confident that they matter and have value. The key worker becomes the child's safe, secure and consistent base to return to, physically and emotionally;

- following and recognising the patterns, tones and rhythms of a child's life, thereby developing a deep understanding of their individual needs. The key worker understands a child's current skills and interests and can engage them in, and extend, their play;

- establishing open communication with a child's parents to ensure the child's needs are met and planned for. The key worker is the person who knows each child, their family and their circumstances and is seen as someone who values what families want to say about their child. Conversely, parents are more likely to spend time talking to someone they feel is committed to caring for their child;

- acting as an advocate for the child, sharing with parents and other practitioners the specific interests and needs of their key children. The key worker has a powerful impact on the wellbeing of their key children and their ability to develop and learn.

Outcomes for the setting of a key worker approach will include improved care and learning for the children, and parents and families who are confident about leaving their children there.

For self-reflection

Have a look at the box below adapted from Manning-Morton and Thorp (2006). If you are a key worker, reflect on your practice using the following as guidelines. Is it time to arrange a meeting with your 'knowledgeable manager or colleague'?

The role of the key worker working with babies and children under three

- Take responsibility for developing secure, trusting relationships with your key children and families.
- Spend time with each key child's family to learn about the child's changing routines, interests and dispositions.
- Settle new key children into the setting gradually, with yourself as the main point of contact for the child and their family.

- Receive and settle your key children as they arrive each day.
- Change and toilet your key children. Use sensitive handling and familiar words/actions/routines.
- Dress and wash your key children. Offer help as needed but also allow for and support growing skills and independence.
- Eat with your key children in small groups.
- Hold key children who are bottle-fed on your lap to feed. Maintain eye contact and conversation.
- Interact with your key children by being physically and emotionally available for them to come back to you by sitting at their level and in close proximity to them.
- Interact with your key children with reciprocal sounds, words, facial expressions and gestures, responding to their individual temperament.
- Provide a secure base by supporting your key children's interests and explorations away from you, perhaps by nodding and smiling as they explore and draw your attention to things.
- Use body language, eye contact and tone of voice to indicate that you are available and interested. Gauge these according to the child's needs and culture.
- Understand and 'contain' children's difficult feelings by gentle holding, providing words for feelings, showing them their expressions in a mirror and showing empathy in a way suited to each child's needs.
- Comfort distressed children by acknowledging their feelings. Offer explanations and reassurance calmly and gently.
- Acknowledge and allow children to express a range of feelings: happiness, anger, joy, distress, excitement, jealousy, disappointment, love.
- Regularly record observations and share them with other staff and the child's family.
- Take responsibility for planning to meet your key children's interests, skills and schemas.
- Take regular opportunities to reflect on the emotional aspects of being a key worker with a skilled, knowledgeable manager or colleague.

Providing the optimum early years environment: the indoor environment

The indoor environment should be one that is developed with the unique and specific needs of babies and children under three in mind. The space available should be designed for comfort, stability and safety, as well as being somewhere where even very young children can explore and take risks. All babies and children under three attending should be happy to be left in their setting. They should perceive the environment as a place that enables them to feel a sense of ownership. There may be boundaries, but their essential needs will be catered for in a setting that is supportive, stimulating and interesting, and where they feel secure that the people within it are trustworthy, reliable and welcoming. Parents should also experience some of the same feelings as their children. They should feel confident that their children will be cared for by practitioners whom they can trust and rely on to ensure that time spent in the environment will be positively and creatively managed and handled. When they pick the children up at the end of the session they will be reassured by a happy, contented, well-adjusted child and a short key worker report on what has happened during the period of care.

Reflecting on current practice

1. How do you know the children who come to your setting are happy to be left?

2. What do you provide upon arrival that reassures both the children and their parents that this is the right setting for them?

3. What procedures do you have in place to communicate with parents both at the beginning and end of their time with you?

4. Is their anything else you could implement to enhance current practice in the above areas in your setting?

Montessori explains that, 'adults can admire their environment; they can remember it and think about it – but a child absorbs it' (1967: 57). When planning an appropriate indoor environment, some key considerations must be addressed:

1. Be creative with natural materials, light and other resources. The setting should be a place of intimacy, challenge and wonder.

2. The setting should reflect some aspects of babies' and children under three's homes, communities and cultures; for example using images and messages that represent home experiences and recognise cultural diversity.

3. Children should feel safe but not over-protected in the environment; the setting must strike a balance between the needs of children to explore independently and the need for safety.

4. Consistency in relation to the layout of the setting is helpful for this age group, as well as allowing for some change to be made where appropriate.

5. The indoor environment benefits from a range of resources, including multisensory and natural resources, as well as familiar items such as comfortable sofas, cushions or favourite toys from the children's home environment.

You can find much more about how to provide the optimum indoor environment in Chapter 5 of this book.

Providing the optimum early years environment: the outdoor environment

It is useful to return to the writings of Robert Owen when considering the outdoor environment. He had something important to say about the value and purpose of outdoor space for us all:

> They will be surrounded by gardens, have abundance of space in all directions to keep the air healthy and pleasant. They will have walks and plantations before them . . . to obtain and preserve health in the best state to ensure happiness, pure air is necessary.
> (*Book of the New Moral World*, 1842)

The outdoor environment is a natural space for learning and development. Being outdoors can have a positive impact on a child's sense of wellbeing, offering them freedom to explore, use their senses and be physically active. Children need to have the support of attentive and engaged adults who are enthusiastic about the outdoors and understand the importance of outdoor learning. They have a natural urge to explore and make sense of the world; therefore an approach to outdoor learning that considers experiences rather than equipment places children at the centre of the provision being made.

> Children can learn to make decisions, solve problems and grow in confidence in their own abilities outdoors and they need plenty of time to investigate their outdoor environment purposefully. They will make predictions about what may happen based on their previous play experiences and test out these ideas and theories.
>
> (DfES, 2007: 5)

Research suggests that if children do not have significant contact with the natural world in their early years then they can become afraid of it. The reluctant child needs to be encouraged; a sensitive practitioner will take them by the hand and walk around the settings outdoor area, exploring the space with them and modelling some of the possibilities. The outdoor environment is where children come into contact with the seasons, the weather, living and non-living things and a different range of sounds. It usually offers more freedom, with room to move, allowing for different movement from that indoors. Consider, for example, the greater physical challenges posed by activities such as digging and riding or pushing wheeled toys. Undertaken in a larger, open space, activities such as these support children in developing their co-ordination and physical strength. Muscles become stronger! Outdoor activities encourage experimentation and practice moving their bodies. When outdoors, children have the freedom to explore and develop their physical boundaries, to take risks and discover this part of their environment with all their senses. Being outside can be liberating for many young children; it is a place where it is 'acceptable' to be active, noisy and messy and where they can work on a large scale. There is an element of awe and wonder about the outdoors environment in that children cannot necessarily predict what might happen, thus providing opportunities for them to experience and develop emotions. Non-prescriptive, heuristic play resources provide open-ended, imaginative opportunities. Using collections of natural objects in this way means that children can use them to fit the play they are working through at the time, rather than the play materials dictating the play.

The outdoor environment is thus full of sources of learning and opens up a different perspective on the indoor environment, even for very young babies who will be interested and intrigued by the sights, smells and sounds around them. As their head and body control develops, they will turn towards what they see or hear and maybe reach out to something that catches their attention. Babies can be safely positioned outside for sleep, giving them fresh air and an environment filled with interesting things to look at when they are awake. As they become more mobile, babies and toddlers will want to explore their outdoors environment, expressing their interests through their emerging physical, communication and language skills. By the age of 2, children become explorers, keen to find out about everything they encounter, such as leaves and twigs, sand and soil. They love to dig and move matter about; sweeping and kicking leaves, for example. This kind of activity helps children to discover the properties of materials and what they will do. By the age of 3 children need opportunities for sustained outdoor play with less familiar resources, such as a parachute, which will encourage collaboration with peers as well as adults. Enhanced communication skills now support this kind of activity.

Creating an appropriate outdoor environment

Good outdoor provision does not rely on expensive equipment. Good provision comes from making the most of the space and resources you have combined with a positive, enthusiastic and engaged attitude from adults. Early years settings need to consider the spaces available to them and how to make the most of them with the resources available.

Ideas for open-ended resources include: different-sized and -shaped logs, poles, sticks and wood shapes, blocks, crates and tyres, natural items such as sand, water, leaves, stones, bark chip, earth, mud, clay, rock, shells, seeds, fabric of different colours, textures and sizes, cloth, tarpaulins, a washing line with clothes pegs, pulleys, baskets, bags, watering cans, containers, pipes of different shapes and lengths, chalks, charcoal, crayons, pens, pencils, brushes with water, paints, large paper or fabric, rollers, tools for digging and planting and caring for plants, tools and benches for woodwork and making, nets, bug pots, magnifiers, binoculars, trays, tanks, dressing-up clothes.

(Adapted from www.norfolk.gov.uk/outdoorlearning)

You can find much more about providing the optimum outdoor environment in Chapter 5 of this book.

Providing the optimum early years environment: the potential impact of the child's home environment in the early years setting

Owen's original message is significant in its acknowledgement of the quality of the home environment and how this might impact on the child's immediate and future outcomes. Of course, 'quality' includes not only the physical environment but also the emotional environment in which children are brought up. Parents play a key role in children's development and learning (Alexander, 2010; Sylva *et al.*, 2010); however, early years practitioners will be aware that this does not necessarily mean that all children experience the same universal upbringing. Recent research has further established, for example, that children from low-income families who, additionally, experience poor parental care can benefit particularly from high-quality childcare (Sylva *et al.*, 2010). Such outcomes would suggest that the period we call childhood is a highly distinct period of human growth requiring careful attention and intervention from a range of different perspectives, including educational, social and political: 'all societies have a universal responsibility to recognise the preschool years as ones in which children should be protected from harm, nurtured in growth, motivated to learn, and equipped to contribute to their society in a multitude of ways' (Renck Jalongo *et al.*, 2004: 144).

Additional factors come into the equation when considering changing work patterns over the past few decades. In Britain, 70 per cent of mothers of 9- to 12-month-old babies now do some paid work, compared with 25 per cent 25 years ago (Layard and Dunn, 2009). Many parents choose to work; some feel they have no choice and simply have to work. In the UK there is currently a major policy drive to encourage as many parents as possible into employment. Whilst the rationale for this might be to reduce child poverty in this country, such a drive can only be successful if parents are provided with a choice of good, affordable childcare. Such settings must be places where they are happy to leave their children. Alexander notes the potential in the early years of a child's life 'for creating sound partnerships between the parents and practitioners who care for and educate their children' (2010: 166). Settings must develop ways to engage effectively with parents in supporting their children in order to be able to thrive in the current progressive and economic climate. Working with parents to develop respectful and trustworthy relationships is thus vital to the success of any setting providing care for babies and children under three. Understanding a child's unique home environment (parental, community and cultural influences) will help the setting support them and their family, target provision and provide an appropriate environment to ensure that learning and development takes place.

Conclusion

This chapter has set the context for the remaining chapters of the book through considering the following key points in relation to what constitutes an appropriate environment for learning. Providing the optimum early years environment takes into consideration the following key points:

- beginning with the individual child;
- the potential benefits of a key worker approach;
- considering the potential for learning within both indoor and outdoor environments;
- taking into account the high level of need and demand for high-quality childcare for babies and children under three;
- understanding the potential impact of the home environment on every child's developmental pathways.

These themes will be interwoven throughout subsequent chapters.

2 The developing child

This chapter gives an overview of different aspects of child development between birth to three years to further set the context for appropriate provision for this age group. Development at this age is rapid but uneven. It is important to bear in mind that children will have different learning needs and that they will develop and learn in different ways and at different rates. In response, the early years practitioner needs to be flexible when thinking about environments appropriate to individual children's stages of development. This chapter summarises some of what is known about how children develop and learn and the implications of this for the early years practitioner. It is important to bear in mind that all areas of learning and development are equally important and interconnected.

It was argued in Chapter 1 that a purpose of early years care and education is to enable each child to achieve higher levels of development through interaction with their physical and social environments. To put this another way, appropriate environments play a pivotal role in supporting and extending the development and learning of babies and children under three. It is therefore essential to start from where each child is, developmentally, in order to provide age-appropriate care and support. This is an age group with unique characteristics, which behaves in certain ways, and which has specialised needs. The principal need for new-born babies is that of calm, for example. The successful early years practitioner must recognise the essential nature of babies and children under three and design learning environments that facilitate the achievement of their developmental goals. Consistency for this age group is vital and hugely important on two counts. First, babies and children under three need a stable, reliable group of caregivers with whom they can form secure relationships. Second, they need consistency in relation to their physical environment; an 'identifiable space whose parameters are regular, dependable and comfortable' (Dimond, 1979: 27). At the same time, they will need opportunities to respond to challenge within the environment. From their early days of playing simple games such as peek-a-boo and hide-and-seek, children will progress to needing real adventure. To be able to venture into the uncharted unknown however, they need the reassurance of the known. An appropriate environment will recognise and provide for these two juxtaposed needs in the developing child.

Contexts for development

1. Cognitive development

The outcome of cognitive development is thinking. However, a young child's ability to think is a process that develops over a prolonged period of time. This is because of the gradual and orderly changes that must occur to ensure their thinking processes become more complex and sophisticated. Piaget, Bruner and Vygotsky all developed cognitive development theories, each emphasising different areas and ideas in relation to a child's development. In addition, both Piaget and Vygotsky were regarded as constructivists. A constructivist approach is one that regards the individual as an active learner who constructs and internalises new concepts, ideas and knowledge based on their own present and past knowledge and experiences. In other words, the learner develops their own hypotheses and builds new knowledge based on what they already know. Following this line of thinking, learning is not fixed and inert, but continually developing. It is clear that theories of cognitive development have profound implications in terms of how the early years practitioner responds to young children. All contemporary theories are agreed that the environment, both physical and social, plays an important role in nurturing children's learning (Ford, 2009). Children's cognitive growth can therefore be enhanced by enriching their early experiences; for example by increasing their access to books and toys, their opportunities for play and their exposure to interaction with more capable others.

Piaget and stages of development

Piaget viewed young children as amateur scientists who carry out simple experiments on their world to discover how it works. He argued that children go through a series of cognitive developments marked by stages. The first two of his four stages of development can be helpful in determining what reasoning power can be expected from a baby or child under three. According to Piaget, infants from birth to 24 months experience the sensory motor stage. Sensory experience for babies and children under three is vital. Throughout this stage, they become more consciously aware of their surroundings, experiencing everything around them through their senses – sight, sound, taste, touch and smell. How often do we see children of this age putting anything and everything in their mouth? Music means movement; seeing invites touching. It is important to remember that children of this age have no protective filter of interpretation, and the environment, along with the resources it provides, must reflect this fact. In order to respond to a child's sense of touch, for example, they need to be able to function in an environment with touch-friendly materials, furnishings and toys.

Piaget's second stage of development, the pre-operational stage, involves children between the ages of 2 and around six or seven years of age. Children learn to manipulate the environment and to represent objects with words. The child develops ability for logical reasoning; however, such logic rests on incomplete knowledge such as explaining the wind by saying that trees make it, or calling all meat 'chicken' because they are familiar with that word and not others, such as pork, beef etc. The specifics of language development are covered later in this chapter.

Vygotsky and sociocultural theory

Vygotsky described the young child as an apprentice for whom cognitive development occurs within social interactions; children are guided into increasingly mature ways of thinking by communicating with more capable others and through interactions with their surrounding culture. This theory, known as sociocultural theory, involves three key features:

1. The cognitive development of children is enhanced when they work in their zone of proximal development (ZPD). The ZPD defines skills and abilities that are in the process of developing – a range of tasks that the

child cannot yet perform independently. To reach the ZPD, children need the help of adults or more competent individuals to support or 'scaffold' them as they are learning new things. Scaffolding instils the skills necessary for independent problem-solving in the future. It is when such social interaction with a more competent member of society occurs that cultural knowledge is transmitted to an individual who, in turn, is able to internalise and incorporate new ideas and concepts into their existing repertoire. Since children are always learning new things, the ZPD changes as new skills are acquired. A child's development cannot therefore be fully understood by a study of the individual alone because the role of significant adults is a highly influential and important factor.

2. The significance of a social context for development. Development, in terms of young children's strategies for and attitudes to learning therefore depends on a combination of interaction with (more experienced) people and tools that a particular culture provides to help children form their view of the world.

3. Knowledge is constructed as a result of the child's active engagement with the environment. It is through such active engagement that a child's thinking develops, as a result of their ability to assimilate and internalise the processes and practices provided by their sociocultural context. The understandings that children develop as a result of their sociocultural background form part of what Bourdieu (1986) calls 'habitus'. Habitus is the lens through which each of us interprets and relates to the world.

Scaffolding and learning 1

Children learn from interactions and conversations with adults and older peers. Through these communications they acquire the cultural 'tools' to aid them in setting and achieving goals and becoming members of communities.

Example
A child learning to walk takes time to learn to do so unaided. Ruby, aged ten months, cannot reach her teddy bear, which she can see sitting on a chair nearby. Her key worker, Emma, notices her standing up by herself on her play mat, somewhat precariously, looking at the bear and pointing to it whilst making noises her key worker interprets

as Ruby indicating that she wants her bear. She asks her, 'Do you want your teddy bear?' Ruby's key worker could go and get the bear for her. Alternatively, Ruby may be able to reach it herself if her key worker walks her whilst holding both her hands. In this way Ruby's key worker provides assistance, her approach acting as a scaffold to Ruby's walking development. She talks to Ruby as she walks her along, saying, 'Shall we go and get your teddy? Emma will walk with you. Let's walk slowly' and, 'How many steps do you think we will take before we reach your teddy bear?' counting every time she places one foot down in front of the other. She praises Ruby, clapping and smiling, telling her, 'Well done! You did it Ruby! You found teddy!', as Ruby reaches the bear.

As Ruby's physical development and co-ordination progress over time, her key worker gradually adjusts the amount of support she gives in response to Ruby's level of performance, which in this case is learning to walk independently. As Ruby becomes more confident in her balance, her key worker goes from holding both hands to gradually holding one hand until eventually she can stop holding that hand until one day Ruby is able to walk to retrieve her teddy bear unassisted.

Discussion point

How else is Ruby's key worker scaffolding her learning?

Bruner

Bruner believes that knowledge and learning are gained most effectively when children learn through personal discovery rather than being 'taught'. He sees children as active, curious and exploratory beings. He also supports the concept of scaffolding, advocating that the adult should assist the child to move from where they are to where they want to go. Such assistance should stem from the child's interests and desires. According to Bruner's model, scaffolding works if the early years practitioner is alert and responsive to a child's learning needs. The practitioner needs to be tuned in to the child's thoughts in a sensitive manner and nurture their learning rather than impose ideas on them. It is almost an intuitive experience, and supports the value and potential impact of a key worker system on a child's development and learning. Bruner's model for understanding the way in which children represent experiences and turn them into knowledge identifies three stages of representation, or modes. Bruner's underlying argument is that cognitive structures mature over time. The child comes to think about and organise the world in an increasingly complex way.

1. The **enactive mode** (representing by doing), which appears first, involves encoding action-based information to store in our memory, or, in other words, representing things by doing. This is an important aspect of early education where the focus is often on the process of learning rather than the product. For example, in the form of movement as a muscle memory, a baby might remember the action of shaking a rattle. The child represents past events through motor responses. Thus a baby might 'shake a rattle' that has just been removed or dropped, as if the movements themselves are expected to produce the rattle sound. Our knowledge for motor skills, such as riding a bike, are represented in the enactive mode. They become automatic through repetition. This first stage of representation can be seen in the way early years practitioners seek to enable children to represent their ideas and experiences actively though play.

2. The next stage, the **iconic mode** (representing by making an image/picture) is one of representation where one thing might stand for another; for example a child using a cardboard box to represent a rocket, or where experiences are represented through recording; for example using photographs or painting. This stage relates to the last six months of Piaget's sensory motor stage and all of the pre-operational stage. During this stage, the child's thinking is dominated by images. Our baby shaking the rattle can now represent his rattle as a visual image.

3. The **symbolic mode** (representing by using symbols/codes) develops last. This is where information is stored in the form of a code or symbol, such as language that starts to influence thought. In the symbolic stage the child can think beyond images. Knowledge is stored primarily through language and numbers. Children use a variety of symbolic codes to express themselves; for example drawing and painting, dancing, imaginative play, making models, language (both written and verbal) and through numbers. Our baby, now a toddler, can say the word 'rattle' when he sees his rattle and picks it up to play with it.

While for Piaget movement between stages was a one-way process, Bruner talks of negotiation and conflict between them. The chosen mode depends on a child's level of experience. With things that are new to us, we are more likely to choose enactive modes of representation or thinking, gradually moving towards symbolic modes as we become more experienced. Unlike Piaget, Bruner proposes that the practitioner should actively intervene to help the child construct new schemas. The practitioner's role is to provide structure, direction, guidance and support, however, not just facts. A key concept of Bruner's theory is the spiral curriculum, where the principles of a concept, topic or subject can be understood at increasingly complex levels.

2. Brain development

The child's brain is remarkably responsive during the first three or four years of life. Advances in neuroscience, evidence from longitudinal development studies and from population studies provide information that early childhood is the period when the child responds to the environment with a tangible malleability that triggers the brain's developing architecture and, through their early experiences, critically shapes who they are as teenagers and adults (Gammage, 2006: 237). Interactions and environments with predictable, responsive care are important to the child's developing brain. Neglect, abuse, and stress can have the opposite effect, causing harm (Zambo, 2008). Factors such as the influence of our early relationships with parents and carers and the immediate external environment we experience as children are therefore extremely important in relation to the importance of providing responsive, age-appropriate early years environments for young children. In relation to the physical environment, for example, research into brain development has confirmed how the actual practice of crawling, handling, looking and communicating builds the neural connections in young brains. Babies and children under three have a strong drive to use their bodies, and children, once they are on the move, learn a great deal through physical experience, inquiry and experimentation. The early years practitioner needs to know how to respond to this phase of the child's development through (a) understanding, and (b) linking what we know of the development of the brain to practice. The early years practitioner who understands the brain and its development in babies and children under three thus confirms (a) their importance and significance to the child throughout this early period of care and (b) their use of developmentally appropriate practice (ibid., 2008).

Brain-based research does not, in itself, introduce new strategies for the early years practitioner, but rather supports connections between what neuroscience tells us and what is already known in relation to good practice for young children. Recent research in the field of neuroscience is often combined with constructivist principles, for example. To illustrate this point, the early years practitioner will recognise the brain-based strategy of immersing the child in meaningful experiences. This is a practice which (a) falls under the umbrella of constructivism, (b) supports the importance of developing and implementing a child-centred curriculum, and (c) supports the importance of developing and implementing a positive learning environment that is appropriate for specific ages and stages (Rushton and Juola-Rushton, 2008). Creating a setting where individual expression and choice are supported provides a learning environment in which children can grow at independent rates. The effective early years practitioner can support brain development by encouraging children to make autonomous discoveries in well-planned environments. Early years practitioners should aim to develop a child-centred learning environment that (a) stimulates the child's interests and (b) optimises the brain's ability to understand, absorb and retain information.

Creating an appropriate environment to support brain development

Babies learn through their senses; they experience their environment through sight, sound, taste, touch and smell. New experiences and stimulation cause different areas of the brain to grow new healthy neural connections. Babies learn through sensory experiences, and the emotional parts of the brain are directly affected by interactions with parents and carers, which includes the early years practitioner. It is important for babies to be responded to in loving, compassionate ways. Touch and infant massage, cuddling with and rocking a baby all help with the emotional connections developing rapidly in the brain. Young children need to feel able to rely on and trust the early years practitioner to soothe them when they are upset. Developing a consistent daily routine helps babies to feel more secure in their surroundings. Repetition of many positive experiences helps to strengthen neural connections in the developing brain to ensure proper brain development.

Babies learn through exploration. Exposing them to stimulating new sensory experiences strengthens connections in the brain. Make sure there are age-appropriate toys to hand. Brightly coloured toys are stimulating, as are those with different textures and patterns. It is important that the early years practitioner interacts with the young child and takes part in their play and exploration.

3. Language development

An appropriate environment for communication and language development is one in which the potential for talk has high status. Babies are born with characteristics that predispose them to be successful language learners. It is important to understand, however, that their language experiences from birth play a significant role in their language development. The significance of the way adults interact with the child at this time should not be underestimated. Children who are not exposed to environments conducive to developing their language and communication skills appropriately are likely to have problems with social, emotional and cognitive development. Whilst there are many reasons why children may have problems learning language, a poor linguistic environment in the early years setting should not be one of them. The way practitioners communicate with babies and young children is therefore a very important part of their role. During the first three years of life, children are:

- developing their knowledge and understanding about how language works;
- developing a range and variety of vocabulary to use;
- learning to speak coherently and with clarity to make themselves understood;
- learning to speak with confidence.

Adults are usually conscious of the language they are using with children, adapting their own register to accommodate the perceived language ability of the child. Early years practitioners, however, need to be acutely aware of their own language use and to be able to change it as necessary. Through taking a reflective approach they can give a range of language-learning opportunities to all the children in their care. When there are a number of children and a lot of work to be undertaken, the amount of time spent interacting with an individual baby or child under three may be limited. Children with fewer opportunities for interaction and for hearing and understanding words and phrases are likely to be delayed in their acquisition of language (Wells, 1986; Harris, 1992). Adopting a key worker approach in the setting may help overcome this potential anomaly by encouraging individual children to effectively 'tune in' to a familiar voice. Furthermore, a key worker who knows their children well will respond and interact with them appropriately. Look at how important this kind of interaction is in relation to overall language development outlined below.

Communicating with babies and children under three

Linguists make a distinction between emergent or pre-verbal language constructions and ones that are fully acquired; the average vocabulary of a two year old is 200–300 words, for example. Whilst a three-year-old child is capable of speaking using complex sentences, their vocabulary, and sometimes their understanding, is still going to be limited. How should the early years practitioner respond? Of relevance here is research into the ways in which adults speak with babies and children under three. One important idea in this area has been the concept of *motherese*, which is about the impact, appropriateness and helpfulness of language interactions, particularly between mothers and their children (Tizard and Hughes, 1984). This is now called child directed speech (CDS) in recognition of the fact that it is not just mothers who modify their speech when talking to young children, but also many key adults involved in a child's life. The early years practitioner is one of those key adults. Peccei (2006) observes that CDS is a natural response to the fact that young children use talk that is semantically and syntactically simple. Therefore, if an adult is to communicate effectively with them they need to use a similar kind of language, a language that the child can understand. Communication between adults and children commensurate with the child's language at different stages is therefore beneficial. The ability of the adult to take into account the limited abilities of the child and adjust their language accordingly so that the child can make sense of them is intuitive for most adults, especially parents/carers and practitioners.

The early years practitioner can provide a number of important conditions for the child such as providing access to a competent user of language, providing opportunities for babies and children under three to develop communication skills and communicating responses that acknowledge the young child as a competent language user. In addition, the practitioner can model (often in an unplanned way) the conventions of language, provide natural feedback on the effectiveness of a child's ability to communicate, scaffold the child's language learning and enable the child to test their current hypotheses about how language works. Specific strategies that can be used to scaffold early language development include: using simple vocabulary, using short phrases or sentences, repeating and emphasising key words or phrases, and using the same words and phrases for repeated everyday activities.

Scaffolding learning 2

Let us go back to the example of Ruby, her teddy bear and her key worker, Emma, from earlier in the chapter. Read the detailed transcript below and note how Emma uses language in the following three ways:

1. breaking the task of reaching the teddy into smaller steps;
2. providing motivation to complete the task;
3. providing feedback about Ruby's progress using some of the scaffolding techniques outlined above.

Emma notices Ruby standing up by herself on her playmat, somewhat precariously, looking at the bear and pointing to it whilst making noises that she interprets as Ruby indicating that she wants her bear.

Emma: Do you want your teddy bear?

Ruby continues to point and make noises, whilst making regular eye contact with Emma.

Emma: Shall we go and get your teddy bear?

Emma holds out her hands to Ruby.

Emma: Would you like Emma to walk with you?

She takes Ruby's hands to support her balance and walks behind her.

Emma: Let's walk slowly. How many steps do you think we will take before we reach your teddy bear?

Emma counts every time Ruby places one foot down in front of the other.

Emma: One…two…three…four…five…

They reach the bear. Ruby leans against the chair for support as Emma lets go of her hands and grabs her bear. Emma praises Ruby, clapping and smiling.

Emma: Well done! You did it, Ruby! You found teddy!

Ruby clasps her bear, touching her face with him and smiles back at Emma.

Emma: You love teddy, don't you Ruby?

Creating an appropriate environment to support communication and early language development

It is important to understand that babies are capable communicators from birth, sensitive to the voice levels and tones of adults around them. It is never too early to start talking to a baby because even if they do not understand the words, the sound and tone of spoken language will reassure them and make them feel safe (Dukes and Smith, 2007). The sound of a familiar voice may engender a response in a baby such as appearing calm and quiet, for example, or by waving their arms and legs around. For reasons such as these it can be helpful for babies to be allocated a key worker in their first early years setting (see Chapter 1). Newborn babies communicate much of the time through crying and it is important to listen to them to understand what they are feeling. In the same way that parents do, the key worker will soon learn to understand the difference between the cry that is saying 'I am hungry' from the one that is saying 'My nappy needs to be changed' or 'I am tired and I need to sleep'.

By the age of three months, babies are able to communicate with adults through facial expressions, slight laughter and new sounds. They learn through imitation (Parker-Rees, 2007). They come to recognise faces, voice and touch. Reading to babies and young children and singing to them, as well as playing imitation games, is therefore valuable. Although not a neuroscientist, Bruner focuses on the importance of the social and playful interactions between adults and babies in supporting the development of language. Games involving rhymes such as 'Peek-a-Boo' and 'Round and Round the Garden' are examples of ways of interacting playfully together. Such games involve actions and consequences that support and reinforce the language of the rhymes, thus creating meaningful contextualised language experiences for the baby.

The growth of language and communication requires a partnership between the child and the environment in which the most significant part of that environment is the adult carer. Both child and adult should have the opportunity to work together to achieve mutual understanding through non-verbal and verbal communication, which is essential for the child's emotional development and wellbeing. Early years practitioners thus need to have a good understanding of the development of communication and the role of the adult in this process.

Reflecting on current practice

Does your setting provide a stimulating, welcoming, language-rich environment? How do you know? Is there anything that you could change that would enhance provision?

You might like to pursue your discussions further once you have read the following section on language development.

Language development from birth to 3: an overview

(Adapted from Dukes and Smith, 2007 and Peccei, 2006)

Activity

Look at the tables below. Throughout all stages, consider the concept of CDS and how you might use this to communicate effectively on a day-to-day basis with the children in your setting.

Age	What to expect	Typical language behaviours	Practitioner responses
0–11 months	A baby who: ● responds to their name ● watches the key worker's face with interest when they talk ● begins to recognise their key worker's voice ● recognises familiar faces and objects ● follows moving objects with their eyes ● is startled by sudden or loud noises ● is soothed by calm or gentle voices or music ● imitates some facial expressions and gestures.	● tries to talk to their key worker using gesture and sound ● smiles at people ● cries, gurgles, grunts and coos to self and others ● uses a special cry when hungry ● begins to laugh and squeal with delight ● reaches or moves towards desired toys and objects ● complains or pulls faces ● babbles to imitate some sounds.	1. Direct your talk to the baby, maintaining eye contact. Keep the youngest babies 8–10 inches from your face when you talk to them to help them focus. Refer to them by name. 2. Mimic the sounds a baby makes to encourage more sounds that will eventually become words. 3. Respond to what babies show interest in, making comments. 4. Play simple games and sing nursery rhymes, lullabies and songs to encourage early listening to voices and sounds. 5. Laugh together.

Age	What to expect	Typical language behaviours	Practitioner responses
8–20 months	A baby who: • understands and follow simple instructions • begins to recognise concepts such as 'up' and 'down' • understands the names of common objects, familiar people and parts of the body • understands the word 'no' • will look at an object when it is pointed out • will respond to simple requests such as 'Show me…[your teddy, your hands]'.	• imitates sounds • begins joining sounds together to create nuances of words • learns to say first real words, usually animals or everyday objects • repeats words said by adults • uses the same word to identify similar objects; for example all animals may be called 'cats' • uses language to gain information by beginning to ask simple questions • begins to use different tones of voice • begins to join in with simple action rhymes • will indicate needs by pointing, gestures and words • refers to themselves by name • knows and can speak 30–40 words and understands many more.	1. Give commentaries on everyday actions. When changing a baby, talk about what you are doing, say the names of the items you are using. Similarly, name clothes and parts of the body when dressing a baby. 2. Look at picture books and photographs together and talk about the people, objects and characters. 3. Use daily routines as opportunities to develop new vocabulary, for example preparing lunch, setting out equipment or tidying-up time. Talk about what you are doing using short sentences. 4. Introduce action songs to a baby; hold their hands and encourage them to join in with the actions. 5. Begin taking turns during simple play, modelling actions such as putting the next building brick on a tower, saying 'Your turn'; 'My turn'. 6. Go for walks in the setting garden or outdoor area and begin to point and name objects that you see, saying 'Look at…' whilst pointing.

Age	What to expect	Typical language behaviours	Practitioner responses
16–26 months	A toddler who: ● turns to look at an adult when spoken to and actively listens ● understands when told not to do something (although they may still go ahead and do it!) ● understands simple 'Show me' requests such as 'Show me your hands' ● understands simple questions and directions such as 'Get your coat,' and 'Where's teddy?' ● understands phrases with two key words such as 'Go and get your coat and hat' ● understands simple instructions such as 'Give me the...' and 'Go to the...'.	● mutters and talks to self when engaged in activity ● uses between 50–200 words or more ● tries to use words that may not yet be clear ● can say 'no' and begins to show possession, for example, 'mine' ● can ask for what they want using words or gestures such as pointing ● puts simple words and gestures together, for example, 'What's that?' whilst pointing ● enjoys singing and will attempt to join in ● asks for specific things by name such as 'juice' ● hands over and names familiar objects and toys on request ● can copy and produce animal sounds ● begins to combine words into meaningful phrases such as 'Bye bye Mummy' or 'more juice' ● begins to use some describing words such as 'big', 'hungry' ● repeats adults, especially the last word in a sentence before absorbing the new word into their own vocabulary.	1. When a child starts to say words use the word, to start a conversation by replying with a simple sentence, e.g. 'Mummy'; 'Yes, Mummy will be back soon'. 2. Make good eye contact during care routines. Provide a running commentary on what you are doing, leaving gaps for the child to fill in the missing words, e.g. 'Let's wash those [hands]!' 3. When a young child talks, stop and give them your full attention. 4. Play together. 5. Carry out simple tasks together such as setting the table for lunch. Use simple instructions and take the opportunity to introduce new vocabulary. 6. Use repetition to affirm your interest and give the child confidence, e.g. 'more juice'; 'Would you like some more juice?' Allow time for a response.

Age	What to expect	Typical language behaviours	Practitioner responses
22–36 months	A toddler or child who: • can follow simple instructions such as 'Bring teddy here' • begins to understand the concept of 'one', for example, when asked to fetch one cup or one brick • understands that objects have uses • can identify everyday objects from pictures and books • will have a favourite storybook • begins to understand and to identify 'big' and 'little' • understands the prepositions 'in', 'on', and 'under' • begins to understand the consequences of their own actions.	• refers to themselves by name • can combine 2–3 words to make a sentence, for example, 'Me do it' • will initiate speaking to adults about everyday things • can repeat simple sentences • will comment to other children during play • uses negatives in phrases such as 'not go' or 'no want' • joins in with some familiar songs and rhymes • uses 'my', 'mine', 'you' and 'me' • can answer simple who, what or where questions • can take two or three turns in a conversation • asks lots of questions • begins to talk about past events, using the past tense, although perhaps with some over-generalisation such as 'drinked' instead of 'drank' • uses plurals.	1. Make jokes out of activities such as putting a coat on to go outside. Say, 'Is this yours?' 'Does it go on your head?' Leave time for the child to respond. 2. Get into the habit of outlining the day's events and activities; ask the child's opinion on what they would like to do. 3. Play turn-taking games, building on the language of sharing. 4. Begin to talk about the future, e.g. 'What shall we do tomorrow?' 'Tomorrow we will do some...[painting].' 5. Ask the child to be your helper and give them small jobs to do that involve simple instructions such as putting the pencils in the pencil pot. 6. Read picture books together, and use visual aids, for example from story sacks, to support the child's retelling of stories.

Non-verbal communication

Non-verbal language such as facial expression, effective eye contact, posture, gesture and interpersonal distance or space is usually interpreted by others as a reliable reflection of how we are feeling (Nowicki and Duke, 2000). Mehrabian (1971) devised a series of experiments dealing with the communication of feelings and attitudes, such as like–dislike. The experiments were designed to compare the influence of verbal and non-verbal cues in face-to-face interactions, leading Mehrabian to conclude that there are three elements in any face-to-face communication; visual clues, tone of voice and actual words. Through Mehrabian's experiments it was found that 55 per cent of the emotional meaning of a message is expressed through visual clues, 38 per cent through tone of voice and only 7 per cent from actual words. For communication to be effective and meaningful, these three parts of the message must support each other in meaning; ambiguity occurs when the words spoken are inconsistent with, say, the tone of voice or body language of the speaker.

Similarly, the practitioner needs to be aware of the messages they are sending out to a child via their use of non-verbal language. It is important to remember that whenever we are around others we are communicating non-verbally whether we want to or not and children need to feel comfortable in the presence of the adults around them. According to Chaplain, 'children are able to interpret the meaningfulness of posture from an early age' (2003: 69). Even locations and positions when talking can be important. For example, it is beneficial when speaking with a young child to drop down to their level, sitting, kneeling or dropping down on one's haunches alongside them. This creates a respectful and friendly demeanour and communicates a far more genuine interest in the child and what they are doing than bending over them.

Of course, babies and children under three use non-verbal communication to give messages about how they feel. Babies, for example, might wave their arms, or kick their legs, stiffen their bodies, arch their backs, or stretch and clench their fingers. Babies also move their gaze away when they are bored.

Activities

1. Go back to the language overview table. Where can you find instances of the importance of non-verbal communication in supporting a child's communication and language development skills?
2. Go back to the transcript between Ruby and Emma. Add in any instances of non-verbal communication between them.
3. Reflect on a recent interaction with one of your children, for example changing a nappy or sharing a song together. What non-verbal communication supported your verbal communications?

Listening and responding to babies

Listening to children is an integral part of understanding what they are feeling and what it is they need from their early years experience:

> Effective listening to babies entails respect and a belief that they are worth listening to. Listening is a two-way process which is not limited to the spoken word. It involves babies being active through sounds, movements and actions of different kinds. Adults need to have the skills to interpret these. In daily encounters, they will make decisions informed by their observations and interactions with babies. They will decide, moment by moment, how best to provide for the babies they care for, sometimes getting involved but at other times leaving babies content in their own explorations.
>
> (Rich, 2004: 2)

Most adults enjoy listening to babies and love their reactions as they engage with them. A baby's smile, for example, is a great sense of real pleasure to many parents; a gurgle, a laugh, a baby sound, hand wave or kick all have the potential for delight and celebration. Adults listen to babies all the time, for example when they are cuddling them, feeding them, changing their nappies or bathing them. There may be complaints from babies when an attentive adult leaves the room or a cuddle ends. Consider the following example.

Charlie came to the setting at the age of 15 months. Through general discussions with his parents, his key worker discovered that they often settled Charlie at night in a rocking chair before putting him in his cot. Charlie and his parents called this his 'little rock'. His key worker thought it might be a good idea if she could find a similar style of chair for the setting. Charlie took great comfort from being held by his key worker in the rocking chair for a short time before a sleep in the afternoon. He understood when he was tired and would look at his key worker and say, 'Little rock', a pattern established at home with his parents. At first his key worker ended the 'little rock' before he was quite ready to go back in his cot. In this instance he would not settle and would call out persistently from the cot, 'Little rock! Little rock!' His key worker soon learnt to gauge when Charlie was almost asleep and ready to be placed in his cot. As she put him down, she would use a reassuring, comforting voice, saying what a lovely little rock they had had together and how she hoped he would have a lovely sleep and that she would be there when he woke up. Charlie's mother, in particular, found his transition into full-time care (having been at home full-time with him up until this point) a little easier to bear through such an understanding response from the key worker.

In this scenario Charlie is:

1. Having his physical needs met.
2. Having his emotional needs met.
3. Developing a strong bond of trust with his key worker.
4. Being cared for appropriately.
5. Being listened to.

Charlie's key worker is:

1. Responding to Charlie's physical needs.
2. Responding to Charlie's emotional needs.
3. Developing a strong bond of trust with Charlie.
4. Caring for Charlie appropriately, not least because of ensured continuity of care approaches between home and setting through discussion with his parents.
5. Listening to Charlie.

Listening to babies in this way helps to ensure that they are valued and feel valued, that they are responded to with care and attention, that their physical, emotional and cognitive needs are met and that their interests and experiences are developed in appropriate ways.

Observing and responding to babies

Babies are deeply interested in the people and the world in which they find themselves. Research has highlighted young children's abilities to imitate the facial expressions, gestures and actions of others (Parker-Rees, 2007). Meltzoff and Moore (1977, cited in Parker-Rees, 2007) discovered the ability of newborn babies to imitate facial expressions, most notably tongue protrusion. Babies can also recognise when their own movements are being imitated, and in choosing to do just what the infant does, adults hold up a 'social mirror' (Rochat, 2004, cited in Parker-Rees, 2007) to the children with whom they interact. Because infants enjoy the companionship and familiarity associated with seeing their own behaviour returned to them with interest, they reward attentive adults with smiles and laughter, shaping the adults' behaviour; when adults find a form of interaction that works, they will therefore be more likely to repeat it.

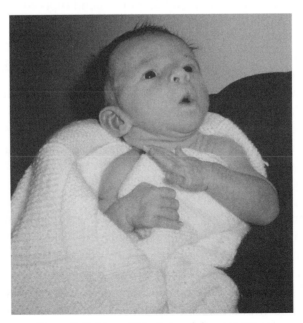

Figure 2 Babies will imitate adult expressions

Summary

Communication begins at birth and can be both verbal and non-verbal. The early years practitioner must model how to be a listener and how to be a communicator. It is important to listen to babies and young children in order to understand and respond to their individual needs. It is also important to allow children to initiate communication and to recognise signals that indicate that the baby or child wishes to communicate, disengage from communication or does not wish to communicate at all. The chapter also highlights the range of communication methods the early years practitioner can use with babies and young children, including non-verbal language. Language develops over a long period; it is a gradual process that must be appropriately supported in order to optimise future outcomes. Language acquisition is likely to be stronger if children are encouraged to become active participants in conversation, if they are encouraged to be questioning, to hypothesise, imagine and wonder. The social and cultural aspects of language development are equally important at this time, as children learn, through talk, to place themselves within a specific social context, and in this way the development of language and identity are closely linked. The impact of what is happening in any child's home life should never be underestimated and it is important for the practitioner to take the time to get to know individual circumstances in order to respond supportively. In order to develop and consolidate their communication skills, young children need:

- to feel safe and secure in their early years environment;
- to build relationships of trust and understanding with their key worker;
- to have access to a wide variety of resources and activities to encourage, develop and support language skills;
- to have constancy and consistency in terms of opportunities and situations in which to develop their language skills. Repetition in routines needs to involve repetition with words and phrases so that language has meaning and familiarity, for example.

In short, babies and children under three need to participate in an environment rich in language opportunities. Language development should be a fundamental goal of all preschool programmes for two reasons: 1. the early childhood years are a critical period in the development of linguistic competence, and 2. language development provides access to future learning, equips the child with an essential communication tool and enables future access to economic and civic participation in society.

4. Social and emotional development

During the first year of life, babies are in the active process of forming social relationships with others (David, 2009). Research has shown that the quality of a baby's early interactions has potential outcomes for the quality of future relationships. One distinct quality of children under three is the development of an individual sense of self. Developing a positive sense of self is also important and impacts on future behaviour, including perceptions of how and what it means to navigate appropriately through life. Bowlby (1969) believed that the earliest bonds formed by babies with their caregivers have a tremendous impact that continues throughout life. Known as attachment theory, he argued that one of the most important bonds a baby can make is with the primary caregiver, a relationship sometimes referred to as the infant–mother attachment relationship as it is typically the mother who fulfils such a role in the baby's early life. Not all babies experience the same quality of early interactions with their mothers, however. Whilst to achieve positive outcomes young children are said to need unconditional acceptance from the significant people in their lives, studies have shown that individual differences in infant–mother attachment security can be attributed to variation in maternal sensitivity (Braungart-Rieker et al., 2001). Mothers of 'secure' babies have been observed to be more reliable, consistent, sensitive and accepting of their child than mothers of insecurely attached babies. In social interactions where a baby's behaviour succeeds in eliciting a positive and sensitive response from the parent, they will feel encouraged to continue the behaviour, however, as suggested in section 3 of this chapter, babies and young children are also able to recognise mismatches between what they hear and a person's body language and such incongruities can confuse them.

Babies often develop a network of attachments made up of all the familiar people with whom they regularly come into contact. It is the quality of such social experiences that are influential in the process of achieving healthy social and emotional development. One such familiar person is a baby's key worker in their early years setting. A crucial factor in a child's social and emotional development, therefore, is the quality of social interactions between the early years practitioner as well as other children in the setting. Research has categorically shown that high-quality preschool provision is significant in its positive effects on young children's intellectual, social and emotional behaviour (Sylva et al., 2010). Where practitioners are warm and responsive to children's individual needs, there will be better outcomes in terms of social and emotional behaviour.

Supporting young children's emotional needs is a key factor in promoting their wellbeing. Children's emotional needs include a sense of security and belonging and having a sense of self-esteem. Emotional needs must be met in order to support a child's developing maturity, independence and autonomy; their ability to learn with confidence, to develop social skills, friendships and rewarding relationships; and their ability to regulate their emotional responses and to respond to the emotional needs of others. Neuroscience confirms the importance of emotional engagement in learning. It follows that once children begin to feel emotionally secure in their early years setting, the scene is set for further learning to take place. Children therefore need to know that the setting is a place where emotions can be expressed. It is the ability to manage some of these emotions through talk that is the challenge both for the individual child and the practitioner.

5. Physical development

Young children have a natural desire to make things happen and to work out how their world works. They use all their senses and apply their physical skills to objects of interest. Their learning grows from the explorations of being able to hold objects and to experiment with actions. Babies have a strong drive to use their bodies. Two- and three-year-olds learn a great deal on the move. Physical movement and skills do matter to young children's development; they engage in a great deal of physical play and sheer joy in using their skills. They need space to move about and hone those skills, for example to walk, run, skip, climb and jump. The use of wheeled toys is a reminder of how play equipment can flexibly support physical development and aspects of co-ordination. A wheeled trolley can be pushed along by a toddler who needs the balance for walking. Soon the trolley is used to carry round teddies, bricks and other toys. The trolley may become a pram or a bus for the teddies. The bricks may need delivering to a building site. An upset child may need a cuddly toy delivered en route. With the child wearing a postman's hat, the trolley becomes a delivery cart that must stop and start as the mail is delivered – all this and having to further think about negotiating the terrain to avoid bumping into peers and furniture too! The point is that young children need to move and they can look and listen when they are using physical skills. Under twos and threes find it hard to stay still, and making them sit 'properly' can disrupt rather than help their powers of concentration. It is important to remember that children can learn on the move.

Gross motor skills are important for the later skills of writing and the development of fine motor skills. Large movements such as playing with ribbons or large swirly movements with brushes are important to support and hone the balance and skills that enable children to control pencils later. Toddlers and two-year-olds like to use and experiment with mark-making items such as a paintbrush, a large crayon or a piece of chalk, and make marks in whatever way they like. The practice builds the basis for the physical skills and intellectual understanding of mark-making in the context of emergent writing. Young children enjoy hands-on activities such as play dough, simple sticking, painting and drawing. They learn through experimentation, investigating materials by poking and pushing, for example, and observing what happens. It is important to remember the purpose of any physical play areas in the setting when creating appropriate environments to address and support the needs of the under-3s (see Chapter 5).

6. Play and development

Early childhood education is underpinned by a strong tradition that regards play as essential to learning and development, for example by setting the context for the development of communication and collaborative skills (Wood and Attfield, 2005; Siraj-Blatchford, 2009). Consider some different forms of play:

- role play;
- imaginative play;
- fantasy play, involving characters and events;
- free-flow play, where children have the choice and freedom to move between play spaces independently;
- structured play with adult involvement;
- heuristic play, which is rooted in young children's natural curiosity; discovery through exploration of objects is key;
- rough-and-tumble play.

Reflecting on current practice

Can you think of any other forms of play? Which are evident in your setting? Which forms of play would you like to develop? What steps do you need to take in order for development to take place?

You might want to look at the chart on perspectives on play and practical implications for the setting on pages 43–6 to support your discussions and considerations.

Global trends can be evidenced in relation to play and its contribution to effective teaching and learning. In England the implementation of the Education Reform Act in 1988 and the subsequent flow of educational policies have fluctuated between an anti- and pro-play ethos. It is important to view these continued debates as positive because they serve to keep play high on educational agendas in policy, research and practice. Again, taking England as an example, the current Early Years Foundation Stage (EYFS) came with a Labour government-endorsed pedagogy of play behind it, exemplified in the following remit: '[The EYFS] must be delivered through planned, purposeful play with a balance of adult-led and child-led activities' (DfES, 2007: 11). Whilst theories regarding the position and purpose of play in the early years curriculum differ in degrees, there is no doubt about the value of play as a tool for gaining experience. Scientists and psychologists have reached the conclusion that since playfulness is present in all humans it must therefore have a biological function; for example, play supports the development of creativity and imagination, which is essential to the development of the flexible and adaptable human brain. It can therefore be surmised that there is a definite relationship between play, learning and development. Play contributes to the holistic development of the child, including the three domains of development: cognitive, affective and psycho-motor. Consideration of the feelings surrounding children's early learning experiences is essential. It is imperative that the early learning experiences offered to the very young respect their natural, playful style of learning. The following table outlines firm perspectives on play and its place in children's development from a range of theorists.

Theorist	Perspective on play	Some practical implications for the setting
Froebel	• Play is part of children's nature and children are happy when playing and learning. • Play fosters emotional wellbeing and is therefore a fundamental source of enjoyment. • Practitioners should not teach by rote but rather encourage self-expression through play.	• The setting should be somewhere where babies and children under three come knowing that they will be able to engage in play, either with their key worker on a one-to-one basis, independently as individuals or in groups of peers. • Babies and children under three need time, space and access to varied resources for play both in the indoor and outdoor environment. • Planning for play should be high on the setting's agenda. It should be flexible, following young children's interests rather than an adult's.
Dewey	• Children learn by doing. They are characterised by curiosity. Experimentation and independent thinking should therefore be fostered.	• It is important to follow a young child's interests when playing. If taking the register becomes taking a fire register, for example, does the child have access to a fireman's hat and tunic? • Problem-solving scenarios are crucial. How to build a house for teddy, for example. Should it necessarily be made from wooden bricks? What about going outside and collecting materials that could be used instead?
Skinner	• After learning children deserve to play. Play should be used as a reward.	• Whilst, at first reading, Skinner's approach may seem inappropriate for children under three, consider, for example, the child who refuses to help tidy up the carpet area so that story time can take place. Encouraging children to take care of their environment is a key consideration from the age of about $2\frac{1}{2}$ to 3.

Theorist	Perspective on play	Some practical implications for the setting
Freud	• Emotional needs can be acknowledged and supported using a range of play activities.	• The provision of role play areas can, in part, help young children to play out their fears and anxieties. • Acknowledge young children's emotional needs through general free play. • Providing art materials can encourage creative expression. • Stories can be used that young children can identify with.
Piaget	• Playing is not the same as learning but can facilitate learning by exposing the child to new experiences in relation to their world. • Play is not a leading source of learning but could actively contribute to these processes. • Play can contribute to the development of problem-solving, creativity, communication and the understanding of social rules. • Children need long, uninterrupted periods of play and exploration.	• Practitioners should create environments where opportunities for play support young children to be active learners, free to explore, combine different materials and create and solve problems through their self-chosen and self-directed initiatives. • Do not feel that a young child should be encouraged to move from an activity and explore what else is available that day in the setting simply because they have been there a long time. If they are engaged, they are happy and they are still learning.

Theorist	Perspective on play	Some practical implications for the setting
Vygotsky	• The value of play is linked to both cognitive and emotional development. • Knowledge and understanding are constructed by the learner through their play experiences. • Children play to escape from reality but at the same time they can get closer to reality, particularly through their role play. • In play children are capable of abstract levels of thinking and often reveal themselves as keen observers and intuitive interpreters of other people's actions, characteristics and behaviour. • Play involves transformational processes in children's knowledge, skills, dispositions and understanding, thus enabling them to move towards higher levels of performance. • Vygotsky's theory of ZPD dictates that the practitioner must engage in some play experiences with children in order to support and facilitate learning.	• The practitioner acts as a model for the child in play, scaffolding their experiences; for example setting the table for breakfast or pouring tea for mummy and daddy bear in their role play cottage. • Observation of what babies and children under three can do and planning appropriate play opportunities that challenge their current capabilities are key.

Theorist	Perspective on play	Some practical implications for the setting
Bruner	• One way in which children seek to represent their ideas and experiences is actively through play.	• Remember that this may include heuristic play where one object represents another, such as a wooden brick for a phone. • Provide plenty of opportunities for 'real life' role play.
Montessorri	• Play experiences begin from birth. • Play is always free-flow. The practitioner's role is to observe.	• Look at the key questions below as a guideline when observing how babies and children under three respond to play activities.

It is important for the early years practitioner to understand the position and purpose of play in young children's development and learning. Potential issues include the following:

• Whilst practitioners are aware that children learn through play, they still sometimes undervalue it.

• Practitioners do not understand how to support children's development through play effectively and extend learning. Remember that play begins from birth; for example with simple peek-a-boo games. Toddlers in their second year of life show the beginnings of imagination that will develop into the complex pretend play of a three- and four-year-old.

• Play can be challenging for practitioners who are concerned with improving the quality of their provision and providing evidence of learning through play.

• Practitioners are anxious about the lack of control in play situations and are uncertain about how to manage a playful environment. By tuning in to play, however, practitioners can ensure that their provision supports the needs and abilities of all children in the setting. Key questions to ask are:

    • What is the child doing?

    • What is play doing for the child?

    • What is happening inside the child's mind?

- What learning processes can we identify?
- How can we use this information to inform and guide our practice?

Research for the DfES led by Janet Moyles found that few early years practitioners could explain why play is an important vehicle for learning.

Activity

Could you explain learning through play?

Conduct the following role play scenario in pairs. One of you is the practitioner, the other the parent of a three-year-old. Explain the purpose of play to the parent in a way that reassures them that their child is learning. Write down some of the key words and phrases you use.

Begin: 'My child tells me that all she did yesterday was play teddy bear's picnic. I'm worried because shouldn't she be doing more than just playing now? She hasn't brought any work home for weeks!'

Try not be too hard on the practitioner!

Figure 3 Babies learn meaningfully through play, both independently and with adult support.

Siraj-Blatchford (2009) argues that play provides a leading context for the acquisition of a child's communication and collaboration skills. She cites those who have shown that a wide range of playful activities progressively engage children in the cultural life of adults and communities; for example Maybin and Woodhead (2003) and Rogoff (2003). Play is important for early learning for many reasons. All of us learn best when we want to do something and we are least likely to learn when we are being made to do something that does not interest us. Children are naturally drawn to play experiences and many concentrate for long periods in their self-chosen play. Play therefore offers children the chance to explore and learn at their own pace and stage of development; it offers children the chance to be in control and to feel competent within relevant, meaningful and open-ended experiences, for example reading and mark-making with a real purpose and without fear of 'getting it wrong'. Through play children are able to meet their own needs and make sense of their world. For them, play involves feelings, ideas, materials, relationships and roles, making connections between one experience and another and representing ideas, objects and environments. Play can provide children with opportunities to use one thing to represent another – for example a block as a mobile phone – and mark-making, effectively laying foundations for the later use of symbols such as letters and numbers to represent ideas. Play encourages creativity and imagination; it is intellectually, socially, emotionally, physically and linguistically challenging and encourages children to work in depth, both alone and with others. It offers them the opportunity to consolidate learning. Finally, children's play enables adults to observe them at their highest level of competence and to see, understand and accommodate their ideas, concerns and interests.

Play and learning?

- Learning has to be active.
- Learning includes repetition/practice/consolidation.
- Learning includes reprocessing spoken or written information.
- Learning involves thinking about thinking.
- Learning involves self assessment and reflection.
- Learning builds upon previous knowledge and work.

Can you see the links with play?

Now choose a resource from your setting. Decide how a child or group of children might play with the resource you have. Consider the following:

1. What would/could a child/group of children learn from playing with it?
2. Could you add anything to the resource to embellish the child's/children's experience?
3. What aspects of learning would you want to observe and record and why?
4. How would you know that learning was taking/had taken place?

Conclusion

Beneficial outcomes for children in care are associated with settings that provide both nurture and support for early learning and development (Snow and Van Hemel, 2008). The years before a child enters formal education are important and irreplaceable in terms of overall development, leading to what constitutes an appropriate environment in which they can learn. Children's behaviour, then, is a developmental area; it is logical that settings should give thought and attention to how behavioural development can be supported alongside other aspects of their development. The overriding goals of the early years practitioner in relation to providing developmentally appropriate care and environments for babies and children under three include:

● beginning with each child as an individual with individual needs;
● supporting children to learn at their own pace; trying to make young children learn something earlier does not help them to learn better. Such pressure could disrupt their confidence, their happiness, and flow of learning;
● following children's interests and enabling opportunities for those interests to be pursued within the learning environment;
● supporting children to develop a view of themselves as happy, enthusiastic learners;

- encouraging children to see the world as an interesting place;
- offering the security of warm relationships, perhaps through a key person system, which links individual practitioners with individual children and their parents or carers;
- expressing affection through words, body language and cuddles. Young children must not be kept at a distance emotionally. Good practice for child protection is fully compatible with expressed affection;
- allocating time to personal care, appreciating a child's gradual development of self-help skills. Regular routines of personal care for young children are not something to hurry through so that they can be moved on to activities viewed as 'educational'. Physical care is an important element of the time shared by the practitioner with babies and children under three;
- developing listening skills. Listening to children is an integral part of understanding what they are feeling and what it is they need from their early years experience;
- supporting children to play and, as they become older, to play considerately with others and to take care of their play/learning environments.

It is important to understand the expected pattern of development for babies and children under three, including the acceptable range and recognised limits. The early years practitioner must distinguish between a child's rate of development (the time-frame in which development takes place) and a child's sequence of development (the order in which development occurs). Whilst there may be an overall pattern of expected development, the rate and sequence of development will be unique to each child.

3 | The policy context

In this chapter, national and international childhood frameworks will be drawn into consideration in terms of (a) statutory provision and (b) the interpretation of such documentation to suit a particular early years setting *in situ* and its unique intake of children. The notion of developing appropriate environments for babies and children under three will be the primary focus for investigation for each of the curricula under discussion. The chapter looks at the Early Years Foundation Stage (EYFS) principle of Enabling Environments in England. Current research, including evidence from the recently published EPPE project, is particularly relevant here, as is a short discussion of the British government's Sure Start policy. In addition, the chapter also looks at two other early years curricula: Reggio Emilio (northern Italy) and Te Whaariki (New Zealand). Both are good examples of the way in which policy and curricula are informed and inform, and are interpreted and negotiated into community-focused and interrelational pedagogies and perspectives of human learning and development. Emerging themes from all three curricula can be drawn on when analysing a setting's practice.

Developing appropriate early childhood environments: some considerations

Since the 1990s, many OECD countries have expanded their early childhood services to develop more coherent and co-ordinated policies (Neuman, 2005). Whilst many countries have reviewed their early childhood systems as a result of this process, the growth of early years services in England has been fuelled both by research into the benefits to children of high-quality early education and a consistent government policy to tackle child poverty, largely through providing childcare to help parents return to work.

Policy interest in the early years has been spurred by research showing that the first few years of life are critical for a child's development and learning (Renck Jalongo et al., 2004; Gammage, 2006). At the same time, an increase in the number of families where both parents work has created a pressing need for good-quality childcare. Consequently, there has been an increasing recognition of the role of early years settings in terms of what their provision can, and should, encompass, including promotion of children's cognitive skills, social skills and support for their working parents. Renck Jalongo et al. (2004) argue that policy frameworks should (a) address the provision of a variety of culturally responsive and demonstrably effective programmes that meet the needs of all families, and (b) include a framework for continuing professional development, establishing adult–child ratios, setting curriculum guidelines and improving and verifying training of practitioners. In Denmark, Finland and Sweden, access to early care and education for children under 7 is a legal right. Here, parents pay low, means-tested fees against their income (Neuman, 2005). French preschool education has a tradition of responding to the holistic needs of individual children in that equal importance is placed on appropriate developmental care and educational needs. Most children in Japan attend preschool and it is in this unique early years setting where social skills and self-control are nurtured through playgroups. In England, recent emphasis has been placed on childcare qualifications, which have been reviewed and upgraded. In addition, the development of multi-agency working and a statutory curriculum that covers the age range birth to 5 are part of a range of mechanisms designed to co-ordinate early years policies and practice.

Learning around the world: three examples

1. England: Sure Start children's centres and the Early Years Foundation Stage

Sure Start is a major policy programme that was announced in 1999. Driven by the then Labour government, a major aim behind the Sure Start initiative was to tackle social exclusion. It was targeted at children and families living in the 20 per cent most disadvantaged neighbourhoods and aimed to help close the gap between the life chances of rich and poor (Sylva *et al.*, 2010). Sure Start was followed by the Neighbourhood Nurseries initiative in 2003, nurseries catering for babies and toddlers located in disadvantaged neighbourhoods so that their parents could work. Finally, the development of Sure Start Children's Centres was offered first to families living in disadvantaged neighbourhoods and then rolled out to some 3,500 communities in the country by 2010. Sure Start is currently based on the premises of establishing holistic services for families and children under 5 under one roof; providing affordable, quality childcare and education; providing health and family support services; and providing services for children and families with special needs. In this way, integrated service provision should meet the needs of all children and families and provide early assessment and intervention for children with additional needs (Baldock *et al.*, 2009). In England, early years services currently operate under the remit of a policy document called *Every Child Matters* (*ECM*), published in 2006. Five principles underlie the still pervasive *ECM* agenda: stay safe, be healthy, enjoy and achieve, achieve economic wellbeing, and make a positive contribution. It is with this context in mind that early years settings in England must develop their provision.

The Early Years Foundation Stage (EYFS) encompasses four main themes: a unique child, positive relationships, learning and development, and enabling environments. Focusing on enabling environments, what does this mean? The EYFS describes principles of practice in relation to the emotional environment, the indoor environment, and the outdoor environment. Taking each of these in turn, the EYFS argues that the emotional environment is created by *all* the people in the setting, the children included. Adults, however, play a key role in that they must ensure that the environment is warm and accepting of everyone, i.e. it must be inclusive. The setting should be a place where babies and children under three can expect empathy from their adult carers and where their emotions and feelings can be accepted and supported. They should feel confident in the environment, willing to try things out, knowing that their achievements will be acknowledged and celebrated. The indoor environment focuses on the provision of a safe, secure and challenging space for children. For babies and children under three this means that the space must be like a second home, providing a place for activity, rest, eating and sleeping. The indoor environment should contain age-appropriate resources that should be well maintained and accessible. Finally, the indoor space should provide for an appropriate range of activities. The outdoor environment supports the premise that being outdoors has a positive impact on children's sense of wellbeing and can support all aspects of their development. It gives children first-hand contact with weather, seasons and the natural world. Outdoor environments offer children freedom to explore, use their senses and be physically active and exuberant.

2. Italy: Reggio Emilia and the role of the environment

Reggio Emilia's approach to the care and education of young children, inspired by the thinking of the psychologist Loris Malaguzzi, is built on the idea of the child as an active agent in his or her own learning, a philosophy that extends to the construction of the curriculum (Jackson and Fawcett, 2009). The organisation of the physical environment is crucial to Reggio Emilia's early childhood programme and is often referred to as the child's 'third teacher'. Preschools are usually filled with indoor plants and vines and are designed to allow for optimum natural light. Classrooms open onto a central piazza, kitchens are open to view and access to the surrounding community is assured through large windows, courtyards and doors to the outside in each classroom. The space is designed to capture the attention of both children and adults through the use of mirrors on the walls, floors and ceilings. Photographs and children's work accompanied by transcriptions of their discussions are on display. These same features characterise the class-rooms, where displays of work are interspersed with objects the children have found and organised alongside classroom materials. The environment therefore informs and engages the viewer. Other supportive elements of the environment include ample space for supplies, which are regularly rearranged to draw attention to their aesthetic features. In each classroom there are studio spaces in the form of a large, centrally located atelier and a smaller mini-atelier, and clearly designated spaces for large- and small-group activities. Throughout the setting, an effort is made to encourage and create opportunities for children to interact. A single dressing-up area is therefore situated in the central piazza; classrooms are connected by phones, passage-ways and windows; and lunch rooms and bathrooms are designed to encourage the concept of community. Among the many innovative ideas and practices associated with the system is that of involving local artists, musi-cians and drama specialists in preschool facilities.

Reggio Emilia's tradition of community support for families with young children expands on Italy's cultural view of children as the collective responsibility of the state. In Reggio Emilia itself, the infant/toddler programme is a vital part of the community, reflected in the high level of financial support. The parents' role is one of involvement at both school and classroom level. Parents are expected to take part in discussions about school policy, child development concerns and curriculum planning and evaluation. Because the majority of parents are employed, meetings are held in the evenings to encourage and facilitate attendance.

3. New Zealand: Te Whaariki

Te Whaariki is a curriculum exemplifying an explicitly bicultural ethos with its philosophical roots embedded within Maori cultural perspectives. It takes a holistic view of the child in the community. The Te Whaariki curriculum is designed for children from birth to school entry. It states that the learning environment in the early childhood years should be different from that in the school sector. The curriculum through the early years is seen as a tapestry (Whaariki means 'woven mat'), with a strong emphasis on play and discovery, allowing children to develop and learn at their own pace. The basis of the curriculum is that it is an amalgamation of different elements beginning with the individual child; the people, places and things in the child's environment – the adults and other children, the physical environment and the resources. From the four principles of empowerment, holistic development, family and community, and relationships, five strands emerge, each feeding into an environment of learning and development. These are:

1. Wellbeing. Children experience an environment where their health is promoted, their emotional wellbeing is nurtured, and they are kept safe from harm.

2. Belonging. Children *and their families* experience an environment where connecting links with the family and wider world are affirmed and extended. They know that they have a place, they feel comfortable with the routines, customs and regular events, and they know the limits and boundaries of acceptable behaviour.

3. Contribution. Children experience an environment where there are equitable opportunities for learning, irrespective of gender, ability, age, ethnicity or background. They are affirmed as individuals and they are encouraged to learn with and alongside others.

4. Communication. Children experience an environment where they develop non-verbal and verbal communication skills for a range of purposes, they experience the stories and symbols of their own and other cultures, and they discover and develop different ways to be creative and expressive.

5. Exploration. Children experience an environment where their play is valued as meaningful learning and the importance of spontaneous play is recognised; they gain confidence in and control of their bodies; they learn strategies for active exploration, thinking and reasoning; and they develop their theories for making sense of the natural, social, physical and material worlds.

Te Whaariki argues that a child's learning environment extends far beyond the immediate setting of the home. Four levels of learning are described, three of which develop the notion of the child's learning environment; Level 1 is about how the learner engages with the learning environment. Level 2 describes immediate learning environments and relationships between them, including home and family, the setting and the people in them. Level 3 concerns the adults' environment and how it influences their capacity to care and educate. Level 4 involves the beliefs and values of New Zealand as a nation concerning children and early childhood care and education.

Emerging themes

What can we as early years practitioners take from these three examples? It is important to remember that each of these curricula believes firmly that early childhood is a distinct and unique stage in human development. It is also clear that knowledge and understanding of the child's whole environment, that which extends between home and school, or in other words their own unique world around them, is seen as important in developing a child's capacity to learn in an age-appropriate way. What must be remembered is that Reggio Emilia and Te Whaariki were never designed to be transferable curricula, nor were they designed as practice to be copied (Gasper, 2010). Both were developed *in situ*, so to speak, to address the needs of particular societies and communities and the individual children therein. What they may do, however, is encourage others to rethink their own approach. Whilst we can certainly learn from their practice, settings need to be aware of what will and what will not transfer; it is surely about building on existing good practice and finding ways to move that practice forwards, if indeed that is what is best for the setting and the community it serves. Emerging themes from all three curricula in relation to appropriate environments for babies and children under three are apparent. These include the following:

- the role of the adult carers in the setting in terms of the atmosphere they create for learning and development;
- developmentally appropriate care;
- inclusion;
- appropriate and stimulating resources;
- the role of parents as partners;
- respect for and understanding of the child's environments beyond that of the setting;
- the importance and value of drawing on a child's culture, interests and what is meaningful to them, including routines, likes and dislikes.

Reflecting on current practice

1. What are the principles behind current practice in relation to how the environment is set up for care and learning at your setting?
2. What can your setting draw on with regard to providing the optimum appropriate environment from the principles and precepts of other early years curricula such as Reggio Emilia and Te Whaariki?

Use the list above as a starting point for key areas for discussion. How could current practice develop as a result of such a review?

Conclusion

This chapter has outlined examples of global approaches to provision for babies and children under three , the focus of which has been on what such approaches have to say in relation to the development of appropriate environments. Following lines of thinking outlined in this book, it is important to remember the uniqueness of international curricula in terms of their particular appropriateness for the communities they serve within their country of origin. At the same time, their usefulness in what might be drawn from different approaches to care cannot be underestimated when considering our own environment for learning. It is therefore important to develop awareness not only of their existence but also aspects of potential application to enhance already established practice.

4 | Developing inclusive practice

The premise for this book suggests that appropriate environments play a pivotal role in supporting and extending the development and learning of babies and children under three. Once we start to think about children's developmental needs, no matter how challenging the physical building may be, we can satisfy their needs in a variety of ways; even in what we might feel are unpromising surroundings we can create appropriate environments for young children. It is all about making the most of the space through organising it well and in response to what we know and understand about the children we care for. Early years settings should set one excellent standard – to meet the physical, emotional, social and cognitive needs of all children within their setting community. To summarise the key points that have been made thus far, babies and children under three need:

- to be valued, listened to and taken seriously;
- opportunities to make connections between their home and the setting and their environments beyond;
- opportunities to develop confidence and self-esteem;
- to feel happy, confident and cared for in their play/learning environments;
- a curriculum that is culturally diverse and relevant;
- to feel included;
- time, space and varied good-quality resources;
- appropriately matched activities and experiences with opportunities for hands-on and brain-on activities;

- opportunities for practice, mastery, consolidation and transferability;
- to play and work alongside skilled, knowledgeable practitioners.

Inclusion thus extends to far more than an issue relating solely to children with special educational needs or with learning difficulties. In the setting, inclusion refers to children, families and staff feeling that they are accepted and valued. Practitioners must work towards respectful relationships that value all children and their families. Inclusion also means access to an appropriate environment; one that will support every child's developmental and learning needs. Within the context of an appropriate environment, the area of inclusion must be addressed.

Reflecting on current practice

1. Looking at the key points listed above in this introduction, how many relate to the provision and development of inclusive practice?
2. Taking each of the points in turn, rate your current provision in terms of your own approach to inclusion.
3. What steps do you need to take in order to develop your inclusive practice?

Developing inclusive policy and practice

A very useful assessment tool to support the rethinking of appropriate prac-tice in this area is the Index for Inclusion: developing play, learning and participation in early years and childcare (Booth *et al.*, 2006). The index is a comprehensive set of evaluative materials developed for early years preschool settings. It is designed to guide them through a series of stages towards developing the optimum inclusive environment for all, no matter how inclusive a setting already perceives itself to be. The index 'can help everyone . . . to find their own next steps to increase the participation in play and learning of the children . . . in their care' (p.1). It includes a planning framework and a set of review materials, including how to produce an inclusive plan. Settings are encouraged to use the index in three ways: 1. to adopt a self-review approach to analyse their cultures, policies and prac-tices and to identify any potential barriers to learning and participation that may occur within any of these areas; 2. to decide their own priorities for change and evaluate their progress; and 3. to use the index to scrutinise existing development policies and review them in the context of whole-setting provision. The index can be ordered from the Centre of Studies on Inclusive Education.

Developing an inclusive environment with a focus on play

Thoughtful arrangements of space and materials can invite children's participation in play and contribute to their efforts to organise and utilise materials, engage peers and persist in play (Doctoroff, 2001). Even small modifications to the environment can support changes in children's behaviour and learning. Some adaptations of the physical environment may be necessary to enable children with disabilities to participate fully in play. Environments designed to enable access for all children convey the message that all types of children can play together and have fun (Allen and Schwartz, 1996). It has already been discussed that arranging the available space into clearly defined areas is helpful. Visible boundaries help children to focus on the play materials in each area, supporting interactions with peers.

Noise levels and lighting

If the setting is too noisy, the potential is there to impede child–child, adult–child and child–adult communication, not only during play but also in other elements of provision. Children need to be able to communicate all their needs and have their needs met: nappy changes, drinks, cuddles and company, for examples. We can all picture the child sat crying in the middle of a noisy room on a play mat feeling distressed, lost and alone, with apparent chaos going on all around him and no adult seeming to pay any attention at all. Some children are particularly sensitive to noise; babies need to sleep peacefully. Noise levels are a special consideration for children with hearing and visual impairments. Despite great steps forward in technology, hearing aids can amplify all background sound and not just relevant sounds. Children with visual impairments are highly dependent on auditory cues. The play space can be separated into noisy and quiet areas. Curtains, carpets and acoustic tiles are all good sound absorbers.

It is important to think about lighting when thinking about where to locate different areas in the available space. Natural lighting is, of course, the best form of light. Blinds can be used to reduce glare from the sunlight and shadows. Lighting conditions are particularly important for visually impaired children and for children with hearing impairments who rely on visual communication language systems such as sign language.

Reflecting on current practice

Looking at a plan view of your setting's, highlight how light works to augment or hinder what goes on in each designated area. Answer the following questions:

1. Does anything need to change?
2. Does anything need to change to support inclusion?

Look at inclusion from the perspective of both the children and the practitioner.

Accessibility of play areas

Children should never be denied access to a play area due to a physical or visual impairment. Pathways should be free of obstructions such as scattered toys or misplaced equipment; any young child is liable to trip; however, children with poor vision and those with physical disabilities are certainly more at risk. Access should not impede those children in wheelchairs or who need walkers.

Reflecting on current practice

Again, looking at the plan of your setting, highlight how current organisation augments or hinders accessibility for children. Does anything need to change to support inclusion? Look at inclusion from the perspective of both the children and the practitioner.

Figure 4 Playing alone; playing together

Play resources

Babies and children under three require a variety and balance of play resources. These should encourage all types of play (dramatic, games, solitary, group, for example) and all aspects of development (motor skills, social competence, cognitive abilities, creativity, language skills and literacy, for example). A setting should also diversify within categories of play resources; blocks and other construction materials that vary in weight, size, material, texture and shape such as Lego™, Duplo™, wooden-unit blocks, magnetic blocks, for example. Think about the range of puzzles your setting currently uses. An inclusive setting must consider its diverse ability levels when selecting resources. This means not only in relation to any children in their care with specific disabilities but also when thinking about and addressing the vast difference between the needs of the age range it caters for, from a newborn baby to the child who is three years old. Resources provided should represent the diversity that children see around them, including diversity of abilities as well as cultural diversity. Representation through play resources in this way promotes self-esteem and attitudes of acceptance and gives out the message that everyone belongs, as well as supporting continuity between the home and setting environment.

Inclusion through the organisation of resources

A well-organised play environment is essential for all children. Visible storage and display of materials, and labels on shelves to indicate where materials can be found can help orientate children to potential play choices as well as help keep the setting tidy. This kind of resource could be placed in low cupboards or on low, open shelves to make access easy and immediate, supporting both the steadily increasing height of the children in the setting's care and also the child with a wheelchair. Consistent placement of resources in the same location will support the visually impaired child. If the positioning of resources is changed, *all* children will need familiarising with the new location. Similarly, if new resources are introduced, all children will need to know where they are to be stored.

Reflecting on current practice

On the plan of your setting, highlight the current arrangements for resources, then answer the following questions:

1. Are resources currently stored in the most logical and accessible places?
2. How are they used to support inclusion?
3. Which need to be accessed independently by the children?
4. Are they able to access them independently?
5. Would some resources be better placed elsewhere, for example to promote children's safety?

Conclusion

This chapter has considered a definition of inclusion that extends beyond children with special educational needs and learning difficulties. Taking play as an example, suggestions have been made to set the scene for in-setting discussions to develop inclusive practice. There is a useful assessment tool called the Index for Inclusion which settings may find helpful if they particularly wish to address the area of inclusive practice.

Creating an appropriate environment: towards a review of practice

The performance of an effective early childhood educator...develops as they continually reflect upon, critically evaluate and moderate their practice to achieve excellence.

(Siraj-Blatchford, 2009: 149)

This chapter supports settings in thinking through how far their existing provision meets the developmental and learning needs of babies and children under three. It incorporates practical ways forward for reviewing a setting's practice in terms of how to assess current provision and develop priorities for the setting development plan. It therefore offers advice on two main counts: 1. the changes a setting may want to make to the child's environment in order to ensure that the experiences offered to babies and children under three are developmentally appropriate; and 2. what those resulting changes might mean to the setting in practical terms. Settings must be confident in their own judgements resulting from such an exercise. The outcome has to be one of knowing that their provision equates to that which constitutes and supports the high-quality appropriate environments that we should all, as early years practitioners, aspire to develop. Many settings undergo this kind of reflective, progressive review on an ongoing basis and, indeed, having worked at an early years setting where this way of working was embedded within the ethos of good practice, it is a good idea to incorporate regular review as one element of a setting development plan.

Chapter 1 explored some of the theory behind the optimum or ideal learning environment. Babies and children under three need to be both encouraged and able to be active in the early years setting. Different areas of learning and development for this age group for which practitioners must provide support include:

- their gross and fine motor development;
- their hand/eye co-ordination;
- their language and communication development – listening and responding;
- their emotional expression and social competence;
- their intellectual skills and understanding;
- their imagination and creative skills.

In addition, early years settings must respond to the stipulations of any statutory curricula or framework within which they are legally bound, the particular needs of the community they serve and the needs of their parents and carers.

Reviewing provision: Where do we start?

The setting's mission statement, or ethos towards supportive learning, needs first to be defined above all other elements of provision. Every setting should have a clearly articulated philosophy and goals that value children, families, cultures and communities. This philosophy should be communicated to the public, reflected in daily practice and revised periodically to reflect how young children grow and learn. The Mission Statement can serve as a useful starting point for fruitful discussion amongst the setting's staff members. What is the purpose of the setting? What are its goals? What are its beliefs? In short, what is at the heart of the setting's approach to supporting babies and children under three? Examples of two fictional mission statements, for the purposes of discussion follow:

Mission statement 1

At Jumping Jacks Day Care Nursery we believe that children must be provided with a safe and stimulating environment in which to grow; a place where they can develop their social and other skills whilst having fun. We believe that they should have the opportunity to play safely and to participate in age-appropriate activities that will lay a foundation for their schooling. We believe that we should encourage the best of diet and exercise habits in order to foster healthy individuals. Above all, we believe that a child decides his or her own pace for doing things. Children at our daycare nursery will not be pushed, merely encouraged. We offer structured sessions that offer our children routine, but which blend with free play time effortlessly.

At Jumping Jacks we therefore aim to:

- provide an environment that is safe, secure and welcoming; one in which learning is facilitated through play;
- help all children make the transition from home to preschool;
- nurture self-confidence and self-esteem, and encourage independence;
- provide a rich play environment where children can explore and experiment without fear of failure;
- promote understanding, kindness and tolerance of others;
- provide an environment where equal opportunities for all takes place, regardless of gender, race, culture or religion;
- provide children with access to the Early Years Foundation Stage and assess their development on a regular basis;
- ensure that the curriculum meets the needs of every child, socially, intellectually, emotionally and physically;
- provide continuity of care through liaison with parents and carers.

Questions for discussion

1. What are the key messages that stand out from Jumping Jacks mission statement?
2. What evidence for your response can you find within what is written?
3. What might be the 'other skills' this mission statement is referring to?

Mission statement 2

At All Stars Day Care Nursery all children will have access to a caring learning community where they are valued for their abilities, accepted in spite of their differences, and where they can be successful in their endeavours. Children are born unique, creative, and capable. The challenge for education is to support these strengths and abilities so that each child can grow and develop lifelong skills of problem-solving, independence, curiosity, co-operation and a positive attitude for learning. Our goal is to join with families in the education of their children. Together we create a community of learners in a supportive, nurturing environment that values our diversity and celebrates our differences. Everyone has an equal right to belong and make choices and to be respected for their uniqueness.

Questions for discussion

1. What are the key messages that stand out from All Stars mission statement?
2. What evidence from your response can you find within what is written?
3. Compare the two example mission statements. Which works best? Why?
4. Could you improve either, or both, statements?
5. Compare the two mission statements with that of your setting. Is there anything you would now like to change as a result of this reflective exercise?

Other considerations for what might be included within a mission statement could be the key principles and values, and even requirements, contained within the early years curriculum to which your early years setting must respond. It may be worth revisiting those key principles and values now and cross-referencing them to your own mission statement. Do they need to be reflected in your mission statement? How can you reflect key principles and values important to you in your own words?

Considering the needs of parents

Any early years setting must be a place where parents are happy to leave their children. Parents will not decide on a setting lightly. For many it will be an anxious time, worrying about whether they are doing the right thing leaving their children when they are so young. They will therefore need to think carefully about the best environment within their means in which to leave their child. What will parents be looking for in an early years setting for their children? Here are some suggestions as to the questions they will be asking:

- How do the caregivers appear? Will they nurture, support and love our children as much as we do? What provision does the setting have/make to ensure this is the case?
- Will the caregivers tell us about our child?
- How will they help us cope with daily separation from our child?
- How will they support us as parents and our child's primary caregivers?

You will see from the range of questions listed that a key element for any early years setting, when looking at the specific needs of parents, is that of establishing a relationship of trust. Parents are their children's primary care-givers; they should not be seen in any other way, even if the setting believes there are inherent difficulties for the family. The key message here is one of respect; put your parents and their needs first and work with them to develop a partnership that ensures continuity of care for them, their children and the setting.

For self-reflection

Exploring your attitude towards parents

- Answer 'yes'/'no'/'sometimes' to the following statements:
- I am a good listener.
- I consider parents' points of view.
- I look at them directly when I speak.
- I ask questions and show that I am interested.

- I make time to see parents.
- I do not interrupt.
- I do not blame them for any difficulties.
- I tell them as much as possible about their child.
- I give advice sensitively.
- Parents can rely on me.

Reviewing current practice

1. What are the specific needs of parents who approach your setting with a view to placing their child in your early years setting?

2. How can you support those parents in reaching a decision?

3. When they visit your setting, what will they see that convinces them that it is the best setting for their child?

4. When they visit your setting, who will they see that convinces them it is the best setting for their child?

5. What does your setting offer parents and their children that is different from anywhere else?

6. How does your setting develop relationships of trust with parents?

7. How does your setting ensure that communication with parents takes place on a daily basis?

8. How do you know that parents are happy with your setting's quality of provision?

9. What are the unique characteristics of the community your setting serves?

10. How are you responding to those unique characteristics? Is there anything else that your setting could offer or that current provision could improve on?

Setting up the setting: appropriate environments

Babies and children under three derive security from an environment that is regular, predictable and constant. The setting should provide defined areas for certain activities and certain types of play, both indoors and outdoors. Arranging the space in this way will help children focus on available materials or resources in that area. It will also encourage play and interactions with peers (Dempsey and Frost, 1993). The available space must be thought about carefully; active play areas should be clearly separated from quiet areas for example. As far as possible, the defined areas should be permanent for this age group, allowing them to learn through familiarity and repetition. Babies and children under three learn from an environment that is reliable and has a clear sense of order. Routines are important.

Setting staff must work as a team to determine achievable and age-appropriate rules and to set clear boundaries based on realistic expectations of baby and toddler behaviour. Children learn through repeated explanation and by experiencing and responding to the rules and structure of the setting. These are best reinforced by the establishment of a regular, ordered environment. Children should be invited to help maintain this order and to understand it. Putting away toys is a major part of the setting day, for example, and it is a good idea to try to slow down the process to give enough time for children to become involved.

Case study: establishing a 'rule'

Aiofe, aged 2, removes a book from the book area and leaves it by the computer. Her key worker notices and says to her, 'Aoife you left your book by the computer'. She points to the book. 'Let's take it back to the book corner where all the other books are.' She indicates the book corner and hands Aoife the book. Taking her hand, Aoife's key worker walks with her in the direction of the book corner. 'We'll take it back to the book corner and put it in the book box where it belongs,' she says. When they reach the book box, her key worker again suggests, 'Let's put it in the book box'. She gently takes hold of a corner of the book and guides Aoife to put it back in the box. As Aoife returns the book, her key worker says, 'Well done Aoife! This is where the books belong. What shall we do next?' Aoife understands 1. she has done something worthy of praise; 2. the best place for books is in the book box in the book corner; 3. things must be put away if you use them; 4. the environment needs her active involvement if it is to support her learning needs. Putting the book away, albeit with support, is a much more effective learning experience for Aoife than having her key worker pick up the book and return it to the book corner for her. Note in this scenario how the key worker consistently repeats instructions and key phrases to support Aoife's language development.

Setting up the setting: appropriate indoor environments

In setting up an appropriate indoor environment in which the emotional, physical, developmental and learning needs of all babies and children under three are met, the setting should aim, where possible, to include a number of distinct, separate and permanent areas for them to access. Suggestions for some of these follow:

1. An active physical play area, called the carpet area in some settings. This is an area that:
    - meets a child's needs for mobility in all directions, from being able to lie and stretch and kick on a play mat to learning to take first steps, to being able to sit and stand and walk around moving a cherished teddy or doll in a pushchair from one place to another;
    - can give children a new perspective such as being above the world, observing others, looking around, looking up or looking down;
    - might require children to take turns or wait briefly;
    - allows children to interact with exuberance, enthusiasm and energy.

2. A manipulative play area that:
    - enables children to find out how things work, to produce effects and solve problems;
    - develops fine motor and construction skills;
    - can allow children to make independent choices in selecting resources;

- can help children take responsibility for caring for their environment and think about the needs of others through learning where items are stored and replacing them after use.

3. A messy play/creative area that:
   - recognises the child's sensory mode of learning about the world;
   - enables children to explore with different media such as water and paint;
   - develops fine and gross motor skills;
   - encourages children to mark-make;
   - allows for social interaction and co-operation;
   - helps children develop respect for the rights of others.

4. A role play area that:
   - encourages the development of a child's sense of self-identity;
   - enables children to take on social roles, to respond to and enact their home experiences;
   - allows children to learn social skills such as turn-taking and playing alongside others;
   - allows children to develop their breadth of vocabulary, and practise conversational language with peers and with adults.

5. An inviting-looking book corner (include some bean bags at least for sitting on, although having a sofa is wonderful) that:
   - encourages children's interest in books, pictures, songs and music;
   - provides somewhere 'cosy' for practitioner–child and child–child interactions with age-appropriate texts;
   - allows the early years practitioner time to assess and develop the child's emerging understandings and skills with language.

6. A quiet play area that:
   - recognises the child's need to relax during the day and to be cosy with an adult as they would be in their own home;
   - provides an essential 'softness' and comfort in the centre;
   - could be used as a place of privacy, a place to retreat to, to be alone and simply to escape the busyness and routine of the setting;

- provides a place for small groups to play together.

7. An area for personal storage that:
- recognises the child's need to belong and to be seen as an individual;
- provides a link between the setting and a child's home;
- encourages the development of independence and self-sufficiency.

8. A curiosity/sensory corner or area that:
- recognises the child's need to discover, explore, touch, examine, listen to and experience a wide range of materials, plants and animals.

9. An eating area that:
- allows babies and children under three to socialise and interact with adults and children in daily routines;
- develops self-help skills and independence.

10. A nappy change/toileting area that:
- can allow a special one-to-one time for babies and children under three and their key worker, recognising the need for personal attention and affection;
- gives the child time to relax and enjoy personal contact, or to look at pictures and mobiles (for example) and to be talked to by an adult.

11. A sleep area that:
- recognises the child's need for a familiar sleep space by providing personal items for comfort and security;
- can accommodate individual sleep patterns and habits;
- should allow early and late sleepers to be placed appropriately;
- can include the planning of a quiet activity for early risers.

12. A dressing and undressing area that:
- recognises a child's need to gradually develop autonomy and independence in self-help tasks;
- allows key workers time to give personal and individual attention.

This list is by no means intended to be exhaustive; however, it may give pointers for development and/or reorganisation of current space. In designing and equipping the setting in this way, key workers should note that the materials and activities provided in each of these areas will be dependent on the ages and developmental needs of the individual children under their care. Non-mobile babies will benefit from a selection of rattles and other noise-makers in the sensory area, for example. In the area for physical play, equipment should be arranged to allow for reaching, kicking and grasping, such as mobiles and other hanging toys. Your setting may have separate rooms for different age ranges and it will be important to discuss organisation and provision as a team to allow for the optimum learning opportunities to take place. However the setting is organised overall, the ultimate goal is to develop a carefully arranged, safe, yet challenging, environment based on a thorough knowledge of the specific needs and development of babies and children under three.

Review exercise

As a staff make a list of the all the indoor areas of your setting. Look at how they correspond with the suggested areas above. Either divide into pairs to look at one or two of the areas together, thus covering all areas. Alternatively, as a whole staff, discuss each area in turn. Ask the following key questions:

1. What is the purpose of the area?
2. What happens there? Why?
3. Which resources are currently available for that area?
4. How are resources used?
5. Is this the most supportive/effective use of available resources?
6. How could the area be improved?
7. Is the area situated in the most appropriate space of the setting? Why/Why not?
8. Is there any money in the budget to provide additional resources that may support development of the area, if indeed it does need developing? Does it simply need to be used in a different way; for example, changes in attitudes, greater understanding of its purpose/how to use it appropriately?
9. Which elements of your discussions need to be included in the setting's development plan? Think about budget, timescale and review.

Setting up the setting: appropriate outdoor environments

In setting up an appropriate outdoor environment in which the emotional, physical, developmental and learning needs of all babies and children under three are met, the setting might wish to consider the following (adapted from White, 2007):

1. Providing opportunities for children to experience a range of natural materials. Sand and soil, for example, are some of the best resources a setting can provide for outdoor play; they are easily found and inexpensive to buy, and easy to store and present in appealing ways. A good supply of multisensory natural materials can:

    *   respond to a child's natural curiosity to explore their world and its make-up;

    *   provide therapeutic play that is emotionally satisfying;

    *   develop intellectual skills – observing detail, sorting, classifying and pattern-making, using representational and symbolic thinking;

    *   provide ways of working with interests;

    *   develop fine and gross motor skills;

    *   support imagination and creativity;

    *   extend a child's breadth of vocabulary through playful interaction and support from key workers modelling key vocabulary and using descriptive phrases.

2. Providing opportunities for children to have real and direct small-scale experiences of the living world around them. Exploring, growing and nurturing plants and wildlife offers children scope for:

    *   learning through doing and a wide range of real experiences with strong emotional contexts;

    *   intimate contact with the natural world;

    *   physical activity and sensory development;

    *   working together, talking and sharing discoveries;

    *   taking responsibility for the wellbeing of living things;

    *   developing an interest in tasting and eating healthy food;

- building foundations for attitudes and interests that can last through life.

3. Providing opportunities for children to explore water outdoors. Water is intriguing for young children, from the baby who tries to catch it in their fingers when it is dropped from a sponge on high, to the child who is fascinated at how it feels on their skin. Playing with water offers children scope for:

    - being wonderfully inventive and imaginative with their ideas and theories, for example seeing how it makes objects move;
    - interacting with it using their whole body and all their senses;
    - exploring water during or after rain/snow/ice, making it even more multisensory;
    - the child to be supported as they learn to make sense of the world around them.

4. Providing opportunities for movement and physical play. Young children love to move; babies kick their arms and legs as they lie on their backs watching an overhead mobile; children want to run before they can walk using a trolley for balance. Providing scope for movement and physical play is important because:

    - movement makes the brain feel energised and moving well brings the enjoyment of being active;
    - activity helps the body develop muscles, bones and tendons. It helps the brain develop sensory pathways. Young children need to move in order to learn;
    - movement and physical competence enable a child to join in with activities that their friends enjoy, and builds relationships; simply running together helps friendships form.

5. Providing opportunities for imaginative and creative play outdoors. Imaginative and creative play includes mark-making, art, drawing, design, construction, problem-solving, music, dance, fantasy or role play, storytelling, and books. Providing scope for imaginative and creative play outdoors is important because:

    - many children find the outdoors a more liberating, flexible and innovative play environment;

- the space allows movement and large-scale working, for example construction in 3-D with large materials;
- it allows the possibility to be active, noisy, multisensory and messy;
- children's natural exuberance when playing musical instruments, singing or dancing is accommodated;
- the natural world supplies many natural starting points for creativity;
- role play scenarios can work better outside where they have greater authenticity and meaning, for example a builder's office or a garden centre;
- participating in outdoor literacy and numeracy activities means that as children get older they do not come to see writing and numbers as indoor 'work' tasks.

6. Providing a covered quiet play area for rest and relaxation. In the summer especially, a simple rug on the ground with soft cushions under a large, leafy tree will suffice. Alternatively, invest in a wooden bench and add soft cushions. Place under a covered area. Your setting may be fortunate enough to have the space for a small, open gazebo. Somewhat similar in principle to the indoors quiet play area, an outdoor quiet play area is important because:

    - it could be used as a place of privacy, a place to retreat to, to be alone and to simply escape the busyness and routine of the setting;
    - it could be used as somewhere to share books quietly together, either on an adult–child or child–child basis;
    - it could provide a place for small groups to play together.

Again, this list is by no means exhaustive but rather intended to give pointers for development and/or reorganisation of current outdoor space. As before, the ultimate goal is to develop a carefully arranged, safe, yet challenging, environment based on a thorough knowledge of the specific needs and development of babies and children under three.

Review exercise

As staff, make a list of all the outdoor areas of your setting. Look at how they correspond with the suggested areas above. Either divide into pairs to look at one or two of the areas together, thus covering all areas. Alternatively, as a whole staff, discuss each area in turn. Ask the following key questions:

1. What is the purpose of the area?
2. What happens there? Why?
3. Which resources are currently available for that area?
4. How are resources used?
5. Is this the most supportive/effective use of available resources?
6. How could the area be improved?
7. Is the area situated in the most appropriate space of the setting? Why/Why not?
8. Is there any money in the budget to provide additional resources that may support development of the area, if indeed it does need developing? Does it simply need to be used in a different way, for example changes in attitudes, greater understanding of its purpose/how to use it appropriately?
9. Which elements of your discussions need to be included in the setting's development plan? Think about budget, timescale and review.

Setting up the setting: extending appropriate environments

Whenever possible, provide opportunities to include outside-world or real-life experiences as part of the setting's provision. Such experiences recognise the special need of the 'childcare' baby or child under three to be part of the everyday world of cleaning, shopping, working, cooking and so on. Extending appropriate environments also includes everyday visits and excursions, for example to post a letter. Whilst children will glean information from and relate to real-life experiences in books and through imaginary play, which is an important element contributing to their development, nothing beats experiencing the 'real thing' for themselves.

Review exercise

What does your setting currently offer in terms of outside-world or real-life experiences? In what ways can you extend or develop these experiences?

Think about children's interests and home life. How can you make greater links between home and the setting in relation to individual children's outside-world or real-life experiences?

Setting up the setting: appropriate environments, resources and storage needs

Resources for early years settings in relation to babies and children under three need to be considered from two aspects: first, there needs to be appropriate provision of resources to meet the particular needs of the babies and children under three. This means, for example, having sufficient and appropriate resources that meet their immediate need for engagement with physical activity, such as climbing, crawling and moving in a range of ways. Continuing the example scenario, children will invariably climb. An indoor climbing structure might prevent the problem of climbing on tables or bookshelves! Settings may need to ensure that there are enough resources available to prevent disputes over favoured items. Modelling appropriate use of resources by practitioners when interacting with the children in their care is also important as it will encourage positive use of them. Thought must be given, however, to elements of heuristic play where one object becomes another for the purposes of the play scene at hand. Support children in this. If a brick becomes a mobile phone, use it in the same way. Resist from saying, 'That's not a phone, it's a brick!' and crushing natural creativity and spontaneity.

The second aspect for consideration in relation to resources concerns storage. Ease of access is important for both staff and children. Shelves and furnishings should not obstruct observation of children by staff or staff communication and should be both high and low enough to allow children to view the room and make play choices. Additionally, the setting needs to find ways of reducing the amount of to-ing and fro-ing that staff are required to do when changing activities or setting up on a daily basis. By ensuring that equipment is close at hand, for example by having resources on open shelves at adult level above the part of the room where it is most likely to be used, or in cupboard units that can be easily opened for children' s use, resources can be provided and packed away easily with a minimum of carrying. As a general rule of thumb, maximise play space by placing all storage on high shelves and planning for everything at floor level to be available to the children.

Review exercise 1

Develop a list of age-appropriate play resources that your setting currently has. You probably have more than you think. You might want to consider natural resources as well as bought ones. Complete the following table:

Age range	Resources (indoor)	Resources (outdoor)	Purpose (learning/ developmental opportunies)	Any gaps?
0–11 months				
8–20 months				
16–26 months				
22–36 months				

Review exercise 2

Look at how resources are being stored at your setting. Does your current storage system work? If not, what needs to be changed? Consider what is stored where, ease of access in relation to areas of the setting and whether you have sufficient storage. Could you simply develop or reorganise your current storage system? If you need to buy new storage equipment, you may have to include this in the setting's development plan. Think about budget, timescale and review.

Setting up the setting: ensuring consistency

Consistency of care for babies and children under three is usually directed at the need for a stable, reliable group of caregivers with whom a child can form secure relationships. Consistency is also required in the setting up of the physical environment where the child enters an identifiable space with regular, dependable and comfortable parameters. Babies and children under three derive security from such an environment. Consistency, however, also extends to continuity that an early years setting can provide between a child's home environment and their care environment. Key workers need to find out as much as possible from parents and carers of young babies before they join the setting so that the routines followed are familiar and comforting. It is important to find out how parents like to communicate with their baby for example. If possible, key workers would benefit from spending time with parents and children in their home environment, where they can be seen engaging in confident, playful interactions. Incorporating such a visit for a new child will ultimately benefit them and their parents as they make the transition from full-time care at home to shared care with the setting.

Review exercise

As a staff discuss the following questions:

1. What does consistency mean in your early years setting?
2. Do you provide consistency for the children in your care? Qualify your response.
3. What are you going to do to improve consistency in your setting?
4. How do you welcome children and parents into the setting on a daily basis?
5. How are you going to create better home-setting links?

A possibility...

Develop an 'All About Me' booklet for parents to fill in details about their child's routines and preferences ahead of their arrival at the setting. The booklet can be used as information for the child's key worker, as a record and as a point from which to develop an appropriate care plan.

Setting up the setting: final considerations for effective early years practice

Communication and collaboration

Effective early years practitioners need to be skilled in, and understand the wider nature of, collaborative practice. Early years work is people-based, highly dependent on interpersonal relationships, on shared values and on understanding how people operate and how they think about their work. Most early years workers are required to work alongside colleagues in a team. In childcare, a team is a group of people that works together to meet the aims of their early years setting. To function well as a team, the team members must be motivated towards common goals, provided with the support and encouragement necessary to achieve these goals and able to communicate effectively. Look at the self-reflection exercise below and rate yourself as a listener.

For self-reflection

My communication skills: How good a listener am I?

Answer 'yes'/'no'/'sometimes' to the following statements:

I look directly at the other person.

I concentrate on what the other person is saying.

I show interest in what the other person is saying.

I ask questions, listen to the answers and reflect back.

I am patient and polite.

I have a friendly, warm, sympathetic attitude.

I know when to stop talking.

I take turns, i.e. ask questions, listen and talk in turn.

Leadership and staff development

All members of staff contribute to the overall ethos of any early years environment. It is important to review every member of staff's professional development on a regular basis. It is not uncommon to set targets and incorporate training courses within staff reviews to support a structure for career development. All parties need to understand that a review is a two-way process; both staff member and manager should come to this process prepared. In order to work effectively in this way, practitioners need to have a panoply of skills at their disposal: the ability to communicate effectively (strong interpersonal skills); the ability to work as part of team, understanding roles and responsibilities; the ability to reflect on and evaluate their own practice alongside the wider reflections of the setting as a whole; and the willingness to respond to change.

Reviewing current practice

1. Do the management team hold high expectations of themselves and others?
2. Do staff have the ability to follow a child-led agenda?
3. Do staff take part in regular and continuing multidisciplinary training?
4. Are all adults involved in the child's educare working in genuine partnership with one another so that they can best meet the challenging needs of both the individual child and their family?

(Abbott and Moylett, 2003: 51)

For final self-reflection

The responsibilities of an early years practitioner

Read the following statements and ask yourself is this you? Are there areas that you need to develop in order to become a more effective early years practitioner?

1. To be an effective early years practitioner I should know how to respect principles of confidentiality. Am I trustworthy?

2. Do I have a commitment to meeting the needs of the children I care for? All children should be treated with respect and dignity, irrespective of their ethnic origin, socioeconomic group, religion or disability.

3. Am I responsible and accountable in the workplace? Do I recognise the expectations of my role and my responsibilities as detailed in my job specification, setting policies and procedures?

4. Do I display a respect for parents and other adults? As part of your professional role, the wishes and views of parents and carers must be respected, even if you disagree with them.

5. Am I able to communicate effectively with team members and other professionals? The importance of clear, constructive communication is a vital element of quality care for babies and children under three.

Conclusion

One of the underlying principles for provision throughout this book has been that babies and children under three need access to high-quality environments appropriate to their age and family circumstances. The book has also assured that changes in practice in terms of provision of high-quality environments are achievable through collaborative reflection, review and a willingness to make appropriate change. Every early years setting has the potential to create a supportive, well-developed, appropriate environment, and in this respect a key message of the book has been about how to make the optimum use of the space and resources available. It is not always about making big changes or spending vast amounts of money, rather taking smaller steps to enhanced provision that might involve a simple reorganisation of resources, for example. This chapter has focused on aspects of provision that must be reviewed, initially on a short-term basis with immediate potential impact in terms of setting improvement, but also with a view to long-term change depending on factors such as the setting's budget. There are many review exercises included, which may at first sight appear daunting; however, each exercise tackles a set area of provision. Together, the exercises are designed to support a holistic review of the setting and can be prioritised by managers and staff collaboratively.

Drawing the threads together

There are essentially seven dimensions of quality (Renck Jalongo *et al.*, 2004) which can be drawn upon in relation to the provision of high-quality, appropriate environments for babies and children under three. Whilst Renck Jalongo *et al.*'s research looks specifically at high-quality provision in early childhood education from a global perspective, the same seven interlinking dimensions are entirely relevant in the context of the content of this book and have been touched on consistently as intertwining themes running throughout each of the previous five chapters. The seven dimensions are as follows:

1. **Sound philosophies and goals.** If a setting's ethos is not based on an appropriate understanding of appropriate care for babies and children under three, and what that means in practice in relation to provision, then the outlook for the children in their care, unfortunately, becomes somewhat bleak. It is good to build philosophies and goals based on the precepts behind what constitutes quality care.

2. **High-quality physical environments.** The focus of this book is the provision of appropriate environments for babies and children under three. This is an area of provision that we have seen is of the utmost importance in supporting a young child's social, emotional and physical development and which is given high credence and space in the three early years curricula examined in Chapter 3. Appropriate environments have been looked at from the perspective of indoor and outdoor provision, as well as organisation of the individuals in charge of care. The impact of the child's home environment is also important when considering the development of appropriate environments within the setting.

3. **A developmentally appropriate and effective pedagogy and curriculum.** The concept of the key worker approach has been put forward for consideration as an appropriate way of organising care for babies and children under three. Consistency for this age group is important and the key worker approach is one way of supporting individual needs and bridging the gap between the child's home and the setting. The benefits of a key worker approach have, additionally, been considered in relation to parents. Elements of effective pedagogy have been explored in relation to the very specific needs of babies and children under three, and it is with a clear understanding of those needs that settings can ensure their provision is appropriate, all of which contributes to an appropriate environment for care.

4. **Attention to basic and special needs.** In an ideal world, all the children in our care would have happy and healthy home lives and circumstances, but, sadly, this is not always the case. All children are entitled to a level of protection and support in their early years environment. The need for an inclusive approach has been outlined in Chapter 4. Basic needs for any child include water, food, shelter, clothing and health care (Renck Jalongo *et al.*, 2004: 145). Sylva *et al.* (2010) report on the findings of the EPPE Project in the United Kingdom, revealing evidence to show that high-quality provision in the early years supports better future outcomes for children with less fortunate backgrounds. By default, all babies and children under three have special needs: the need for attention, the need for support, for someone to feed them, to dress them, to play with them. Then, of course, there are children for whom special needs means something very different, a line of enquiry not pursued to any great extent in these pages but a response to whom must also be considered by some settings.

5. **Respect for families and communities.** It has been shown that the appropriateness of the early years environment should reflect the idiosyncratic nature of the community it serves. An example of how this works in practice can be seen in the ideology behind the Sure Start initiative in England. The book also supports an ethos of home–school liaison and makes suggestions for settings in relation to working successfully and happily with parents for the benefit of each child in their care.

6. **Professionally prepared teachers and staff.** Looking after babies and children under three must be seen as a vocation, and supported as such. Those working with babies and children under three require 'a heart for

children and a commitment to caring' (Renck Jalongo *et al.*, 2004: 146). Babies and children under three need to be cared for by professionals who are in tune with their specific needs, who know how to listen to, respond to and communicate with them. They need to be with carers who know how to respond to their social, emotional and developmental needs and who can develop a correspondingly appropriate environment in which they make progress. It has been argued that all members of staff in any early years setting contribute to the overall ethos of the environment; collaborative practice is essential. Qualifications are a consideration, although not a specific line of enquiry followed in these pages.

7. **Rigorous provision evaluation.** Chapter 5 of this book looks at a review of practice and calls for a regular, reflective and ongoing approach to evaluating provision. Taking the setting's philosophies and goals (dimension 1) as the starting point, suggestions are made as to how to develop the provision that is currently being offered. It is not necessarily a case of buying expensive new resources; a major philosophy of the book encourages settings to look at existing provision with a view to ensuring that space and resources available are organised and used in the optimum way.

Final thoughts

Whilst the content of this book is by no means exhaustive in terms of overall provision for babies and children under three, the purpose has been to exemplify the nature of, the rationale behind, and the value of, appropriate environments for this age group. The book has highlighted the necessity of understanding the contexts in which babies and children under three are enabled to thrive. Babies and children under three need safe but challenging environments in which to learn about their world and develop successfully within it. They are unique individuals with great potential and a natural zest for discovery. Those of us fortunate to work with them find ourselves in a privileged position.

References

Abbott, L. and Moylett, H. (2003) *Working with the Under Threes: Responding to Children's Needs.* London: Open University Press.

Alexander, R. (ed.) (2010) *Children, Their World, Their Education. Final report and recommendations of the Cambridge Primary Review.* Oxford: Routledge.

Allen, K. E. and Schwartz, I. S. (1996) *The Exceptional Child: Inclusion in Early Childhood Education.* Albany, NY: Delmar.

Baldock, P., Fitzgerald, D. and Kay, J. (2009) *Understanding Early Years Policy*, 2nd edn. London: Sage.

Booth, T., Ainscow, M. and Kingston, D. (2006) *Index for Inclusion: Developing Play, Learning and Participation in Early Years and Childcare.* Bristol: Centre for Studies in Inclusive Education.

Bourdieu, P. (1986) *Distinction: A Social Critique of the Judgement of Taste.* London: Routledge.

Bowlby, J. (1969) *Attachment and loss (vol. 1).* New York: Basic Books.

Braungart-Rieker, J., Garwood, M. M., Powers, B. P. and Wang, X. (2001) Parental sensitivity, infant affect and affect regulation: predictors of later attachment. *Child Development*, 72 (1): 252–70.

Chaplain, R. (2003) *Teaching without Disruption in the Primary School.* London: RoutledgeFalmer.

David, T. (2009) Young children's social and emotional development, in T. Maynard and N. Thomas (eds) *An Introduction to Early Childhood Studies*, 2nd edn. London: Sage.

David, T., Goouch, K., Powell, S. and Abbott, L. (2003) *Birth to Three*

Matters: A Review of the Literature Compiled to Inform the Framework to Support Children in their Earliest Years. Research Report 444. London: DfES Publications.

Dempsey, J. D. and Frost, J. L. (1993) Play environments in early childhood, in B. Spodek (ed.) *Handbook of Research on the Education of Young Children.* New York: Macmillan.

DfES (2007) *The Early Years Foundation Stage Effective Practice: Outdoor Learning.* Nottingham: Department for Education and Skills.

Dimond, E. (1979) From trust to autonomy: planning day care space for infants and toddlers, in E. Jones (ed.) *Supporting the Growth of Infants, Toddlers and Parents.* Pacific Oaks, CA: Pacific Oaks College and Children's School.

Doctoroff, S. (2001) Adapting the physical environment to meet the needs of all young children for play. *Early Childhood Education Journal,* 29 (2): 105–9.

Dukes, C. and Smith, M. (2007) *Developing Pre-school Communication and Language.* London: Sage.

Ford, R. M. (2009) Thinking and cognitive development in children, in T. Maynard and N. Thomas (eds) *An Introduction to Early Childhood Studies,* 2nd edn. London: Sage.

Gammage, P. (2006) Early childhood education and care: politics, policies and possibilities. *Early Years,* 26 (3): 235–48.

Gaspar, M. (2010) *Multi-agency Working in the Early Years Challenges and Opportunities.* London: Sage.

Harrison, L. (1989) *Planning Appropriate Learning Environments for Children Under Three.* Revised edition 1996: Australian Early Childhood Association.

Holt, J. C. (1989) *Learning all the Time.* TN: Da Capo Press.

Jackson, S. and Fawcett, M. (2009) Early childhood policy and services, in T. Maynard and N. Thomas (eds) *An Introduction to Early Childhood Studies,* 2nd edn. London: Sage.

Layard, R. and Dunn, J. (2009) *A Good Childhood: Searching for Values in a Competitive Age.* London: Penguin Books.

Li, Y. L. (2006) Classroom organization: understanding the context in which children are expected to learn. *Early Childhood Education Journal,* 34 (1): 37–43.

Manning-Morton, J. and Thorp, M. (2006) *Key Times. A Framework for Developing High Quality Provision for Children from Birth to Three.* Maidenhead: Open University Press.

Maybin, J. and Woodhead, M. (eds) (2003) *Childhoods in Context.* Chichester: John Wiley.

Mehrabian, A. (1971) *Silent Messages.* Belmont, CA: Wadsworth.

Montessori, M. (1967) *The Absorbent Mind.* New York: Holt, Rinehart and Winston.

Moyles, J. (1997) Just for fun? The child as active learner and meaning maker, in N. Kitson and R. Merry (eds) *Teaching in the Primary School a Learning Relationship.* London: Routledge.

Neuman, M. J. (2005) Governance of early childhood education and care: recent developments in OECD countries. *Early Years*, 25 (2): 129–41.

Noddings, N. (2002) *Starting at Home: Care and Social Policy.* Berkeley, CA: University of California Press.

Nowicki, S. and Duke, M. (2000) *Helping the Child who Doesn't Fit In.* Atlanta, GA: Peachtree.

Parker-Rees, R. (2007) Liking to be liked: imitation, familiarity and pedagogy in the first years of life. *Early Years*, 27 (1): 3–17.

Peccei, J. S. (ed.) (2006) *Child Language: A Resource Book for Students.* London: Routledge.

Renck Jalongo, M., Fennimore, B. S., Pattnaik, J., Laverick, D. M., Brewster, J. and Mutuku, M. (2004) Blended perspectives: a global vision for high-quality early childhood education. *Early Childhood Education Journal*, 32 (3): 143–55.

Rich, D. (2004) *Listening to Babies.* London: National Children's Bureau.

Rogoff, B. (2003) *The Cultural Nature of Human Development.* Oxford: Oxford University Press.

Rushton, S. and Juola-Rushton, A. (2008) Classroom learning environment, brain research and the no child left behind initiative: 6 years later. *Early Childhood Education Journal*, 36: 87–92.

Snow, C. E. and Van Hemel, S. B. (eds) (2008) *Early Childhood Assessment: Why, What, and How.* National Research Council.

Sylva, K., Melhuish, E., Sammons, P., Siraj-Blatchford, I. and Taggart, B. (2010) *Early Childhood Matters: Evidence From the Effective Pre-school and Primary Education Project.* Oxford: Routledge.

Siraj-Blatchford, I. (2009) Early childhood education, in T. Maynard and N. Thomas (eds) *An Introduction to Early Childhood Studies*, 2nd edn. London: Sage.

Tizard, B. and Hughes, M. (1984) *Young Children Learning.* Oxford: Blackwell Publishing.

Wells, G. (1986) *The Meaning Makers: Children Learning Language and Using Language to Learn.* London: Hodder & Stoughton.

White, J. (2007) *Creating an Outdoor Learning Environment for the Early Years. Early Years Update*, December.

Wood, E. and Attfield, J. (2005) *Play, Learning and the Early Childhood Curriculum*, 2nd edn. London: Sage.

Zambo, D. (2008) Childcare workers' knowledge about the brain and developmentally appropriate practice. *Early Childhood Education Journal*, 35: 571–7.

Index